AF269533

Roberto Burle Marx Lectures

Landscape as Art and Urbanism

Edited by
Gareth Doherty

Photographs by
Leonardo Finotti

Lars Müller Publishers

To Haruyoshi Ono

I spent the summer of 1996 in Roberto Burle Marx's studio in Rio de Janeiro studying his work and influences. It was two years after Burle Marx's death. As a parting gift, Haruyoshi Ono, Burle Marx's successor as director of the studio, presented me a photocopy of every lecture they then had that Burle Marx had delivered in English in various institutions around the world. At that time, I had little to no Portuguese and they felt this was the one way I could carry something of Roberto with me and get to know him better after I returned to university. This original set of lectures, which were distilled into nine, plus three English translations later found in the studio's archive, form the basis of this volume.

When I revisited the lectures several years later, I remembered how much they had influenced me at the time as a student of landscape architecture. I was most impressed by their consideration of the relationality of color, form, light, sound, texture, and volumes. Burle Marx discusses the urban and social agenda of his work, to which I responded strongly. Often presented as a self-indulgent artist, obsessed with doing what *he* wanted, Burle Marx's dimension of social responsibility was most surprising. So too was the discussion of the creative process. The popular assumption is that Roberto Burle Marx had a creative genius that came out of nowhere and can't be understood, and that his office has access to his secret recipe. But he says outright in one lecture in this collection, "There are some principles that guide us; they must not, however, be mistaken for formulas." [p. 173]

There are indeed certain principles to Burle Marx's nonsymmetrical curves, and the formal aspects of Burle Marx's work. However, he was supported by a large team, and a whole assemblage of relationships, and that's one of the reasons the office has continued to practice many years after Burle Marx departed this world. I would like to briefly share a couple of impressions from those few months in 1996. It was winter in Rio then, but the Rio winter is a lot like summer.

The first thing that struck me about the studio, officially known as Burle Marx & Cia. Ltda., was that the office was in a family house. The 19th-century villa was located on Rua Cardoso Júnior in a leafy neighborhood of Rio de Janeiro, called Laranjeiras, the "Orange Grove," a once fashionable area of the city. The interior was largely as it must have been when it was used as a family home. The reception desk was in the hallway, meetings held in the parlor, and the midday meal was cooked in the kitchen by the housekeeper, Dona Francisca, who was always very nice to me. Meals were served in the dining room where even the tablecloth was designed by Burle Marx. The studio space could be found in a rear extension, the upper floor of which housed a commercial gallery for paintings and art works by Burle Marx. The walls of the house were filled with his paintings.

One cannot help but wonder if the family atmosphere contributed to the success of the practice. It is a family that exists well beyond Rio to encompass a whole network of people who at one point or another passed through the doors of Burle Marx and Company. In the studio, the staff ate meals together and this, I later came to realize, was an important part of the ethos of the studio. Everyone had access to everyone. Random issues were discussed, ideas generated, plans made, and solutions found over *feijoada* and rice, and *mousse de maracujá* (passion fruit mousse). The hospitality of the office, and openness to discussion, was very important for the working of the office, and derived from Roberto's gregarious and kind persona.

The studio kept in touch with the plant nursery in the *chácara* (small farm) that provided many of the plants for his landscapes. There was a connection to the Sítio, Burle Marx's home of 45 years, where he painted and experimented with compositions and juxtapositions of plants and forms. There was also a maintenance team who kept the landscapes in check long after they were constructed. These related enterprises partly explained why the office was so prolific. Roberto Burle Marx is often credited with designing over three thousand landscape projects in his lifetime–that's three projects a week on average. Whatever the actual number of landscapes designed, the creative office consisted not just in the design office, the villa, in which the nonsymmetrical curves were worked out over yellow tracing paper; but in the Sítio as a place of research; the *chácara,* the plant nursery and place of production; and the mobile maintenance crew, all in one full service. This was not just about efficiency. It was all about creativity and the constant to-and-fro of the design process.

Although I was in Rio two years after Burle Marx had passed away, his absence was still sorely felt in the office. The office arranged for me to visit many of his gardens and landscapes in and around Rio de Janeiro and São Paulo, sometimes staying overnight. I would talk with the users and owners of the spaces as much as I could. I draw from these experiences in the introduction as well as conversations with Haruyoshi Ono.

I am struck at how the office has continued even after Roberto's passing, and more recently after the passing of Haruyoshi, to whom this book is dedicated. By all accounts Roberto had an extremely strong personality. It takes equally strong personalities to live up to that reputation and keep it going, and I am very happy that a new generation, Isabela, Júlio, Gustavo, and team, are continuing that pioneering work.

Gareth Doherty

On Burle Marx and His Lectures

Gareth Doherty

On being awarded the Fine Arts Medal of the American Institute of Architects in 1965, Roberto Burle Marx was recognized as the "real creator of the modern garden."[1] The significance of his landscape architecture is often attributed to his use of abstract curves and forms, which rarely employ symmetry, and his use of tropical, mainly indigenous Brazilian flora. This collection of a dozen of Burle Marx's lectures, most of which have never before been published in English, offers new insights into Burle Marx's thoughts and works. Distinct sets of relationships emerge across the lectures, showing Burle Marx not just as a gardener, artist, and botanist, but as a landscape architect whose ambition was to bring radical change to cities and society.

Speaking shortly after Burle Marx's death in 1994, Sir Geoffrey Jellicoe, himself one of the leading landscape architects of the 20th century, praised Burle Marx as "the top landscape architect in the world," and then proceeded to advise: "He's held that position for fifty years or so." The power and vitality that lie behind Burle Marx's work is legendary; "Now what is this thing that Burle Marx has got?"Jellicoe pondered. "And I'm still thinking hard on what it is, but it's there all right."[2]

Burle Marx has too often been regarded as primarily a painter and plant collector, who fused these two passions into the art of garden design. He is sometimes likened to Gertrude Jekyll and William Robinson, who "went into the woods" and saw native plants and thought, "why not use them in gardens?"[3] Indeed, as a Brazilian, Burle Marx sought to create a gardening style particularly suited to his home country, using native flora. "Although we know that the Brazilian flora is one of the richest and most surprising in the world, our plant vocabulary for gardens, up to the first quarter of this century, was exceedingly small," he tells us in *Finding a Garden Style to Meet Contemporary Needs.*

While Burle Marx has been the focus of many articles, books, essays, exhibitions, interviews, and even television programs, very few of Burle Marx's own words have been published, especially in English.[4] This volume offers the opportunity to allow Burle Marx's words to illustrate some of the intentions behind his work and in the process understand a little more about what it is that "Burle Marx has got."

The introduction is arranged in three parts: first, a summary of Burle Marx's background; second, an outline of his major landscapes–well-documented elsewhere but included here for context; and third, an overview of the main themes running through the lectures. Burle Marx emerges as a landscape architect who, while firmly rooted in the composition, form, materiality, sound, texture, and volume of the spaces he designed, was driven by a passionate agenda to improve and conserve landscapes and consequently the lives of the people who live in them.

1. Brazilian and German Roots

At the time of Roberto Burle Marx's birth in São Paulo in 1909, Brazil was emerging as an independent republic in the wake of Portuguese colonialism and the collapse of the Brazilian Empire. The nation was fervently searching for its identity. Burle Marx was the third son of a German immigrant father and a Brazilian mother. The family enjoyed relative privilege, and Roberto was introduced to the arts and to gardening from an early age. Roberto's father, Wilhelm Marx, a successful businessman, was a distant relative of Karl Marx, and his mother, Cecilia Burle, hailed from Pernambuco, a state in northeastern Brazil.[5] Following Brazilian tradition, the children carried the double surname Burle Marx. The children spoke Portuguese with their mother and German with their father and during family meals. Roberto was to master six languages in his lifetime.[6]

In 1913, the Burle Marx family moved from the Villa Fortunata on São Paulo's Avenida Paulista to the Leme area of Rio de Janeiro, close to Copacabana, in what was the capital city at that time. Roberto was introduced to gardening at the third house occupied by the family, the Fazenda do Leme, on what is now the Rua General Ribeiro da Costa, three blocks from Copacabana Beach. The young Roberto, following the example of Cecilia, turned to the large family garden for his hobby. In fact, Burle Marx attributed his love of gardening to his two mothers. Roberto had a close relationship with the housekeeper, Anna Piascek, calling her his "second mother"; Anna stayed in his home until her death at age 103. Anna introduced Roberto to the joys of sowing seeds and observing their growth. He learned flower arranging from Cecilia, whom in *Finding a Garden Style to Meet Contemporary Needs* he describes as "my Pernambucan mother." Together they hybridized plants. Roberto bred a distinct purple tone of *tinhorão* (*Caladium*) which as we will see led directly to his first garden commission. These skills and passions were to stay with him all his life. He imported seeds from Europe, and his father arranged a subscription to *Gartenschönheit,* the well-known German gardening magazine.[7] The journal, which existed between the late 1920s and the 1940s, was richly illustrated with black-and-white photographs of plants, planting designs, and plans. In *Finding a Garden Style to Meet Contemporary Needs,* Burle Marx credits the images from the magazine as having inspired his first landscapes.

The Burle Marx family found their recreation in music and good company. Cecilia conveyed a great love of music to her six children; William Howard Adams, who curated an exhibition of Burle Marx's work at the Museum of Modern Art in New York in 1991, refers to Cecilia's teaching Roberto the leitmotif from Wagner's *Tristan und Isolde*.[8] Indeed, the eldest child, Walter, was a prodigy on the piano and gave his first public concert at the age of nine.[9] The Burle Marx family enjoyed convivial Sunday lunches, and regularly had no fewer than forty people at the house, a tradition Roberto upheld throughout his life.

Roberto was a delicate child, having had tuberculosis at an early age and as a consequence, he received private instruction rather than attend school.[10] He excelled at singing, and one of the reasons the Burle Marx family set off for Germany in 1928 for eighteen months was so that Roberto could receive proper voice instruction. He duly trained in Berlin and was told by his teacher that he had the most perfect student's voice he had ever heard.[11] Europe in the late 1920s, coupled with exposure to art and music, classical and contemporary, had a tremendous influence on the young Burle Marx. One of the greatest impacts was the tradition of plant collecting: at the Dahlem Botanical Gardens in Berlin, Burle Marx was confronted with the wealth of native Brazilian flora and wondered why not use them in Brazilian gardens. However, this epiphany was not enough to immediately change his direction in life: Burle Marx in "The Last Interview," with his good friend and colleague Conrad Hamerman, pointed out that he was still uncertain at that time about his future: "I didn't know whether I was going to dedicate myself to music or to the plastic arts."[12]

Burle Marx took drawing lessons at the school of Elise Degner Klemm, who introduced Roberto to an abundance of cultural events: "Our lives revolved around the theater, the concerts, the opera, Wagner, Richard Strauss....The whole musical panorama I knew well."[13] It was Wilhelm Marx's intention that his family have a thorough "culture bath."[14] A German tutor, Eva Busse, had been hired for Siegfried, the youngest, but felt a special affinity toward Roberto and introduced him to drama, museums, and art galleries. Busse encouraged Roberto to read *Les Misérables, Madame Bovary,* and *Salammbô* in French along with Dostoyevsky in German: this appears to be the only record of Burle Marx's tastes in literature.[15]

Burle Marx, in the end, decided not to pursue a career in music, as he had intended, but to study painting instead: "And I saw the first major exhibit of Van Gogh's work. It filled me with enthusiasm; those paintings–that violent expression–invaded my whole being! I realized painting would have to be my medium."[16] Roberto recalled a visit to a gallery just before he left Berlin, where he was introduced to the works of Picasso, Klee, and Matisse for the first time. "It was a great shock. It was so brutal. I couldn't forget... I got a stroke, an indigestion. It took me a very long time to assimilate."[17]

After the family returned to Brazil in 1930, Burle Marx enrolled in the Escola de Belas Artes (School of Fine Arts) in Rio de Janeiro. He had initially enrolled in architecture, but promptly transferred to painting at the suggestion of Lúcio Costa.[18] Costa, a neighbor and lifelong friend of Burle Marx's, was briefly director of the Escola de Belas Artes, and was

a   Ministry of Education and Health
Rio de Janeiro, 1938
Plan for the roof garden. Gouache, 41⅜ × 20½ in
(105.5 × 52 cm)

b   Praça de Casa Forte
    Recife, ca. 1935
    Chinese ink on paper, 27 × 19¼ in (64 × 49 cm)

many years later to be the planner of the new capital, Brasília. Burle Marx studied under the distinguished Brazilian painter Candido Portinari, and the Austrian painter Leo Putz. At the same time, and still living at home in Leme, Burle Marx also began experimenting with the family garden, introducing Brazilian plants to compare and contrast them, as a painter would with the paint on his palette.

2.   The Work

Burle Marx received his first landscape commission in 1932 at the age of 23, as a result of Lúcio Costa's visiting the family garden. Burle Marx recalls Costa's visit in *Finding a Garden Style to Meet Contemporary Needs:* "When he […] saw a flower bed I had planted with white *tinhorão* (*Caladium*) and deep purple-brown coleus foliage: and he decided that the painter I was then studying to become […] should have a chance to be the landscape architect of the new style." Costa immediately invited Roberto to design a garden for a house he was designing with his collaborator, the architect Gregori Warchavchik,[19] for a family called Schwartz.

The Schwartz garden led to Burle Marx's appointment as director of parks in Recife, the capital of Pernambuco state, through a similar serendipitous encounter. The governor of Pernambuco was passing the Schwartz garden, and was so impressed that he inquired after who had designed it. He called personally to the Burle Marx house and invited Roberto to the nearby Copacabana Palace Hotel for an interview.[20] Roberto moved to Recife and the three municipal gardens, or parks, which he subsequently designed, allowed him the opportunity to prove himself. [photos 5–8] Like many young designers, he wanted to show the breadth of his knowledge. In *Finding a Garden Style to Meet Contemporary Needs* he remarks: "Into the designing of these I put everything I knew." [p. 184] A newspaper article following the same lecture reports that when speaking of this early work Burle Marx conceded, "I did a salad, but I didn't do a garden."[21] He included water features in the parks, and in the Praça de Casa Forte [photo 8] he included *Victoria regia*[22] water lilies with their 6-foot-wide (2 meters) leaves for the first time in a public space in Brazil. In another park, the Euclides da Cunha Square [photo 7], he created a cactus garden that did not need much irrigation. His references came from *Gartenschönheit* rather than from the European garden tradition common in Brazil at that time, and this brought him praise and critique in equal measure. Traces of the parks exist to this day, although as with many of Burle Marx's landscape projects, they have not been maintained as well as he might have hoped. [fig. b]

The Roof Garden for the Ministry of Education and Health in Rio de Janeiro, designed in 1938, earned Burle Marx worldwide acclaim. [photos 1 and 2, fig. a] The building was a collaboration among a group of young Brazilian

architects headed by Lúcio Costa and including Oscar Niemeyer with
Le Corbusier as a consultant. It remains one of the finest examples of
modern architecture in Brazil. Burle Marx's roof gardens employed tropical
plantings in sinuous form. This style, with large-scale plantings of
contrasting colors and textures, was to stay with Burle Marx all his life,
although he progressed from using many plants and organic curves in
his early work to a smaller number of plants and more geometric forms
later in life. The plan of this roof garden was widely exhibited, the bold
color contrasts no doubt adding to the appeal. Walter Gropius allegedly
once declared that he liked Burle Marx's gardens but could not understand
his plans.[23] The plans are gouaches, painted painstakingly in the office.
They are completely flat, showing the juxtaposition of the various elements
through color and composition. Generally speaking, a plan would take
about two weeks to color, and as a consequence they were only produced
for exhibitions and publications. [fig. a]

At this time Burle Marx was primarily a painter who looked to the
landscape for his painting materials. As he states in *Concepts in Landscape
Composition,* "I decided to use natural topography as a surface for
composition and the elements of nature, mineral and vegetable, as materials
for the plastic organization, the very thing that other artists try to do on
canvas with paint and brush." [p. 88] Burle Marx's painting style is akin to that
of Cézanne and Matisse, and is significant for its interplay of color and
form rather than for the subject. Burle Marx claimed that his approach to
art could largely be explained in terms of the impact of cubism and
abstraction on his generation. Although Burle Marx was later to suggest
that his curves were influenced by the curves of rivers flowing through
the Brazilian landscape (see *Finding a Garden Style to Meet Contemporary
Needs,* for instance), he, and his curves, were influenced by many sources
including Picasso, Miró, and Kandinsky, as well as the landscape and rivers.
As he tells us in *Concepts in Landscape Composition,* "The juxtaposition
of the plastic attributes of those aesthetic movements with natural elements
created the attraction to a new experience." [p. 88] Haruyoshi Ono, his
successor, elaborated further: "He had an open mind and looked [at]
everything and had a good memory. When we traveled by airplane he looked
there and saw the shapes. He was always looking at the place, the form,
the colors, the dark, and the light."[24]

While Burle Marx's interest in plants dates from childhood and his interest
in specifically Brazilian plants from his time in Germany, his collaboration
with the Brazilian botanist and plant collector Henrique Lahmeyer de Mello
Barreto was of great importance in Burle Marx's growth as a landscape
architect. Mello Barreto was interested in the study of plants in their natural
habitat. He was a perfect partner for Burle Marx, who sought to use native
plants not just for their own sake, but for their relationships to each other and
to their environment. The two men went on many plant-hunting expeditions

c   Ibirapuera Park
São Paulo, 1954
Perspective view of unrealized raised-path garden.
Gouache, 39 × 59 in (100 × 151.2 cm)

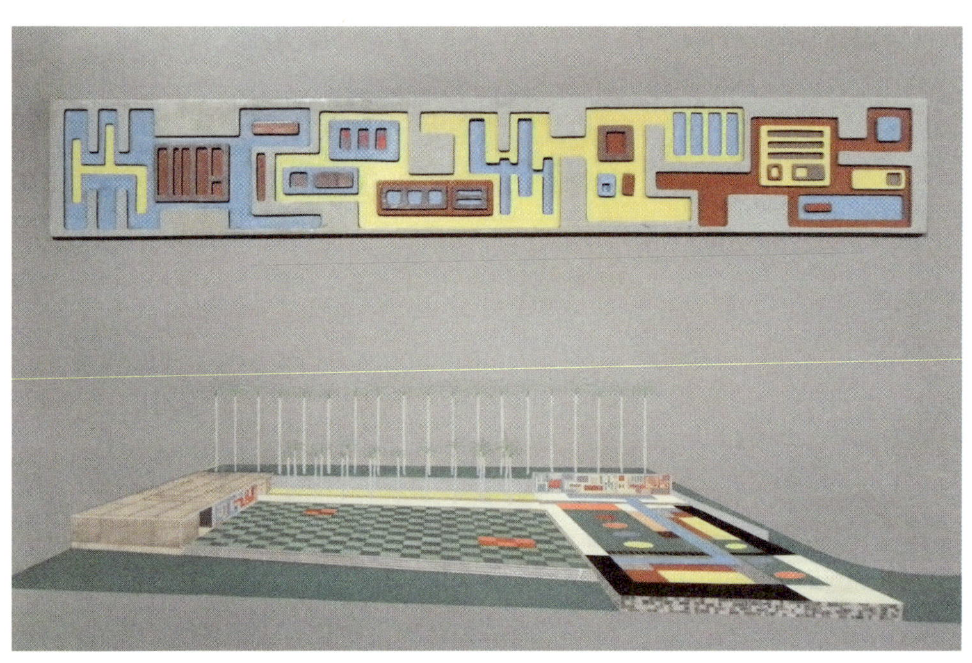

d   Parque Burle Marx (formerly Pignatari Residence)
São Paulo, 1956
Maquette and perspective view. Maquette,
paint on panel, 48½ × 59⅜ in (123.2 × 150.8 cm)

together in the Brazilian interior, especially during the 1940s. In *Gardens and Ecology,* Burle Marx recalls an impression from their fieldwork: "Climbing the mountains, after traveling over extensive grasslands, I came across a grayish spot of rocks and as I came closer a completely new world opened up to me. An extraordinary society seemed to have been created to form a complete reciprocal harmony." [p. 138] The concept of the social relationships of plants is a recurrent theme across Burle Marx's lectures.

Their most noted collaboration was a park in Araxá, a spa town in Minas Gerais, around 1943. [photos 3 and 4] Together they planned a series of rock gardens, using a different rock type in each, accompanied with its corresponding flora. As a response to problems with the upkeep of his early parks in Recife, Burle Marx included plants that could look after themselves. The plans were never fully executed, whether for economic reasons or because they were considered too radical for their day. A few years later, Burle Marx and Mello Barreto collaborated on a layout for the Rio de Janeiro Zoological Gardens.

In 1948 Burle Marx designed the gardens for the Fazenda Marambaia (then known as the Odette Monteiro Residence), near Petrópolis, about 1.5 hours north of Rio. The site is surrounded by mountains and the dramatic setting makes one consider whether it is the landscape or the garden that is so overwhelming; perhaps it is both. Burle Marx describes his process for integrating this garden with the surrounding landscape in *Finding a Garden Style to Meet Contemporary Needs,* telling that he accomplished the union by placing in the garden "groups of boulders with plant groups that repeat the rock vegetation of the region, while the boulders echo the sheer granite of the mountain." [p. 191] In the same lecture, Burle Marx stresses that the most important point in a garden "is the human contact with ordered nature that must never be lost sight of." [p. 195] He claimed to have considered the scale and proportions of the Fazenda Marambaia "in such a manner as not to lose sight of the man who walks its paths, crosses its lake by the stepping-stones, or stands beside its trees. Thus, he will not be dwarfed by the size of the garden nor lose his feeling of a right to his position in space." [p. 195]

This play with scale where his landscapes become intermediaries between the scale of the human figure and the landscape beyond is repeated in many of his projects, except where the garden is completely enclosed. Burle Marx received an award for the Odette Monteiro Garden at the International Exhibition of Architecture in São Paulo in 1953, at which Walter Gropius was also honored.

In 1949, together with his younger brother Siegfried, Roberto bought Sítio Santo Antonio da Bica, a small farm of about 200 acres (80 hectares) outside the village of Guaratiba, about 30 miles (45 kilometers) south of Rio. This was to be his home for the rest of his life. [photos 11, 12, 57 and 58] There, Burle Marx painted, sculpted, planted, and experimented with the garden. Roberto surrounded himself with art: his own, and Brazilian folk art. Roberto had, at last, space to expand his collection of tropical plants. Siegfried ran the *chácara* beside the Sítio where the plants were propagated for the landscapes Roberto designed. They maintained their partnership until the Sítio was bequeathed to the Brazilian nation in 1985. The new estate provided the excuse to go on many more plant-hunting expeditions, where he encountered several of the biomes he describes in *Landscapes of Brazil.* Burle Marx's plant collection amounted to 3,500 species at one stage, and was significant for *Araceae* and native Brazilian plants. Over the years, Roberto used thousands of different plants in his landscapes, always allowing the natural form of the plant to take shape. Among his favorites were bromeliads, such as *Vriesea imperialis* and *Philodendrons. Hohenbergia burle-marxii* was Burle Marx's favorite out of the thirty or so plants named for him, some discovered by him and others by his friends and colleagues, such as Mello Barreto.[25]

The garden of the Sítio, which he worked on for the rest of his life, is his expression of self, circumstance, and experimentation on the landscape. He declares in *The Garden as a Way of Life* that landscape architecture is an art form, "the result of a web of concepts and knowledge, woven by the life of the artist himself, through his experiences, doubts, anguishes, tests, mistakes, and successes." [p. 132] Just as he saw plants as being related to one another, Burle Marx acknowledged the multiple relationships and experiences that accumulate to inform design decisions. More than any other landscape he worked on, the Sítio was an expression of Burle Marx's life experiences onto a singular physical space.

Following these early successes came many commissions, publications, lectures, and exhibitions. Burle Marx's garden for Olivo Gomes at São José dos Campos in São Paulo state in 1950, adjacent to a house designed by Rino Levi, was well publicized at the time. [photo 21] The garden is now converted into a public park and known as Parque da Cidade. One of the most celebrated projects from this period was the uncompleted plan for the Ibirapuera Park in São Paulo, on which Burle Marx collaborated with Oscar Niemeyer. [fig. c] Ibirapuera Park was the first specially commissioned municipal park in São Paulo, conceived in 1954 for the 400th anniversary of the city. The Garden of the Francisco Pignatari Residence (now the Parque Burle Marx) in São Paulo (1956) was also a collaboration with Niemeyer and initially a private garden. [fig. d] It is now, as its name suggests, a public park. The large concrete murals and water features employed in this landscape were to become recurrent themes in his work. In later projects the murals were to become almost three-dimensional with planting beds incorporated into them. Public projects from this time include the Largo do Machado in Rio (1948) [photos 15 and 16], and the Praça Terreiro de Jesus in Salvador da Bahia (1952) [photos 13 and 14], two modest yet centrally located urban squares with abstract patterned surfaces, which were to become one of Burle Marx's trademarks.

The Parque del Este (1961) is one of Burle Marx's best known public landscape projects. [photos 54–56] Sited on a former coffee plantation on what was formerly the edge of Caracas, the park consists of about 200 acres (80 hectares), and has three main types of space: a large open lawn, a series of smaller spaces enclosed by woodland, and a series of geometric courtyards. The larger open space may initially call to mind English Romantic parks, contrasting with the more enclosed wooded spaces, yet sympathetic transitions between them are unified by undulating pathways. There is a concert stage near the main entrance, and from there one can choose to walk directly to the romantic landscape or turn left to go through a series of geometric gardens where cool colors contrast with blazing reds of the tiled walls. The park is programmed with various activities: aviaries, crocodile enclosures, fish ponds, a monkey island, walled gardens, flowing lawns, cafés, and a boating lake all cater to diverse interests throughout the rest of the park. While not constructed totally as Burle Marx had intended, this park surely sets out to achieve what he called for in *Finding a Garden Style to Meet Contemporary Needs,* "The garden will have a social as well as an educational and scientific character, where its functions will be determined by the aspirations of an era, linked to man's aesthetic and ethical conduct." [p. 172] The plants for the park were carefully considered, with a preference toward indigenous plants suited to the location, soil, and climate. In *Finding a Garden Style to Meet Contemporary Needs* he tells us, "In any environment, a garden should be designed according to existing topography, and planted in accordance with the climatic and soil conditions of the region." [p. 181] But, he qualifies, "When we find a gap in our plant vocabulary, and this can be filled by an imported exotic plant that harmonizes with the landscape, I think that this plant should be used." [p. 183] Less than half of the plants in the Parque del Este were native to Venezuela; Burle Marx preferred ecological groupings of acclimatized plants rather than take the risk of juxtaposing the wrong form or volume.[26] [fig. e]

Flamengo Park (1954–1964) [photos 51–53] is the result of a huge (and by today's environmental metrics, questionable) landfill project along the length of Guanabara Bay, just south of Rio's city center. The park was planned by a group of designers led by the self-trained architect Maria Carlota Costallat de Macedo Soares, with Burle Marx as landscape architect. The park contains more than three thousand species of trees, grouped ecologically, and chosen as much for their color when viewed from above—to provide interest from the many apartment buildings lining the bay, not to mention planes arriving at the adjacent Santos Dumont Airport—as from their interest from below.[27] Affonso Reidy's Museum of Modern Art (MAM) is situated at the northern end of the park. The garden around the MAM building was one of Burle Marx's most famous gardens, dating from 1954. The distinctive patterned lawn, created using two varieties of *Stenotaphrum* grass, is no longer distinguishable. The proximity of this project to the city center brought with it unexpected pressures for nighttime use. Burle Marx discusses the issue with the lighting in *The Problem of Garden Lighting,* complaining that the "huge lampposts were placed [...] breaking the scale of the park and the landscape of Guanabara Bay, without bringing any new idea in lighting and without any imagination or technical criteria in their indiscriminate placement." [p. 201] Perhaps this was one of the reasons he became so interested in landscape lighting in later life. [fig. f]

After these large urban projects, and a temporary decline in his artistic and professional output in the mid-1960s, in 1968 Burle Marx formed what was to become a very successful partnership with two younger architects, José Tabacow (until 1982) and Haruyoshi Ono, who was to inherit Burle Marx & Cia. Ltda. on Burle Marx's death in 1994, and became his successor as director of the studio. Projects from 1968 onward include various works in Brasília, Copacabana Beachfront, the Banca Safra Headquarters in São Paulo, and the exquisite Fazenda Vargem Grande.

For over one hundred years before it was planned, it had been under consideration to build a new capital for Brazil. Brasília was planned and to a large degree built during the presidency of Juscelino Kubitschek (1956–1961), and as such, as Jellicoe and Jellicoe point out in 1976, it represents a "moment in time"; they declare it a "monument to architecture (rather than society)."[28] Planned by Lúcio Costa, the principal architect was Oscar Niemeyer. Both had worked closely with Le Corbusier on the design for the Ministry of Education and Health in Rio in the 1930s. Despite his position as Brazil's foremost landscape architect at the time, Roberto Burle Marx was surprisingly not invited at the initial stages of the design of Brasília. It is often suggested this is because of his disagreement with President Kubitschek 10 years beforehand. While Kubitschek was Mayor of Belo Horizonte, he found himself unable to pay Burle Marx for his work on the Pampulha Casino Complex, now the Museum of Art, an early collaboration with Niemeyer.[29] Bruno Zevi suggests it is because Burle Marx did not have the ability to deal with the complexity and scale of such a large urban landscape, which is disingenuous given his work on Flamengo Park and the Parque del Este.[30] But the architect, Hans Broos, who knew Burle Marx, says it was due to Niemeyer, who had little time for Burle Marx ever since their collaboration on the Ibirapuera Park in São Paulo.[31] Whatever the reason, Brasília is very much the poorer for a lack of comprehensive landscape architecture.

Burle Marx received the commission for the gardens of Itamaraty Palace, the Ministry of Foreign Affairs, in 1965, after President Kubitschek left office. [photo 24] The exterior garden is a water garden, with strategically placed, organically shaped islands of plants and sculpture. There are also indoor gardens planted with shade-tolerant plants. It is situated close to the Congress buildings and across the Monumental Axis from the Ministry of Justice, where Burle Marx also designed the garden. Around that time, he designed the courtyard and open spaces of Superquadra 308 Sul, one of the most iconic residential blocks in Brasília.

The Triangular Garden at the Ministry of the Army (1970) was one of three gardens that Burle Marx created for buildings designed by Niemeyer in Brasília. [photo 25] The garden is sited away from the other ministry buildings, at the other end of the Monumental Axis from the Congress. Water is the main feature, and the form of the lake reflects the form of the paving patterns. This garden is characterized by the crystalline sculptures protruding from the lake. Haruyoshi Ono's description of the design process for the park provides an insight to their working habits: "In a lot of cases he just gave a drawing and some person made the model or made a drawing. The sculptures in Brasília, he made a rough draft and then I made the model, and made it for real from the model."[32] Also notable is the abstract paving, a technique that was to culminate in Copacabana.

The Copacabana Beachfront in Rio, dating from 1970, was like Flamengo Park before it, the result of another huge landfill project, where the beachfront was moved out creating a new hard surface between the building line and the beach. [photos 26–31] With its undulating tessellated stripes, it graphically displays and celebrates the patterned pavements he began using in earlier squares. He uses traditional Portuguese paving materials—hand-cut basalt setts of about 2 inches by 2 inches (5 × 5 centimeters), surfaces generally in white, reddish-brown, and black—in a thoroughly abstract way. He also retains the Portuguese wave pattern adjacent to the beach, although he made it parallel to the sea, whereas previously sections of the beachfront were perpendicular and others parallel to the sea's waves.[33] The wavy design—often misattributed to Burle Marx—was adapted from the Portuguese wave pattern used to commemorate floods in Lisbon in the 18th century.[34] The distorted forms of the deciduous *Terminalia catappa* trees look particularly striking in August, although they are no longer allowed in Brazilian public spaces, since they are of African origin and only native plants can now be planted in Brazilian streetscapes. The *Terminalia* was one of the species that filled a void in Brazilian flora for Burle Marx. The Júlio de Noronha Square in Leme, at the northern end of Copacabana, near Burle Marx's former home, completes the beachfront. Although the square was only implemented in 1992, the final design closely resembles an early sketch (ca. 1970) discovered in a file in the office of Burle Marx & Cia. Ltda.

The roof garden of the Banca Safra Headquarters, on the Avenida Paulista in São Paulo (1983), was created on the ninth floor of the headquarters of the Banca Safra. [photo 32] The structure of the building did not allow for large quantities of soil to be placed there. Burle Marx improvised with the use of artificial stone and potted plants, combining them in his distinct way. This garden is simple and masterful—Burle Marx at his best.

Of all his landscapes, the Fazenda Vargem Grande, near Areias in São Paulo state (1979–1991), embodies the essence of Burle Marx. [photos 17 and 39] He doesn't discuss it in his lectures, as most of the lectures had been written before this garden was designed, but it is worth mentioning as a culmination of the lectures in some ways. Haruyoshi Ono ranked this garden among Burle Marx's finest landscapes.[35] It is a geometric garden imposed on a hillside. The client, Clemente Gomes, was a friend of Burle Marx and was in fact the son of Olivo Gomes, for whom Burle Marx designed the garden at São José dos Campos in 1950. Burle Marx worked on the garden of the Fazenda Vargem Grande from 1979 to 1991, although construction took place over a shorter period. [fig. g]

Set in a very sparsely populated valley, the Fazenda Vargem Grande is a former coffee plantation. The life of the garden lies in the water channels bringing water from the mountains. Burle Marx used this water to create a series of pools and waterfalls. The sights and sounds of water abound. It is this domination and the preponderance of geometric shapes in the garden that makes one question the concept of movement that had until now seemed so central to Burle Marx's style. The bromeliad garden or Garden of Volumes using desert plants is in stark contrast to the water theme and was intended to be so. The scale of the garden mediates between the surrounding landscape and the human body. In daylight this works very well. At nighttime the hills disappear in the darkness and the floodlights light only the immediate garden and trees, thereby reducing the scale and altering the proportions. Now, the water feature is very big, very dominant. The sound of frogs dominates. The sound is rather like a hammering noise, but Burle Marx described it as follows: "At night you will have here a marvelous concert with the frogs and the animals that are living here. The frogs here have very strong voices, sometimes as baritone, sometimes like a Caruso,[36] they can sing in a beautiful way."[37] In the morning, when the surrounding hills and landscape reappear, the garden has different proportions: the garden fits perfectly into its landscape. The use and relationships of plants are wonderfully evocative. The garden is in many ways composed like a painting, strong in colors and textures but also including sound and volume. Haruyoshi Ono described Burle Marx's design approach as follows: "First he put together the functions of the garden: 'There's the playground, swimming pool…' and then he linked them together. Then he started to put the plants, like a painting.…"[38] Burle Marx employed various elements in the composition of his landscapes, such as plants, rocks, and water, and was open to new and experimental materials. In his early work he liked to juxtapose many materials, plants, and textures. In later life he was much more restrained. In *The Function of the Garden,* he admits that "to make a synthesis, to say the maximum one can say with a minimum of means, is difficult.…" [p. 172]

While Burle Marx says there are no formulas, there are a few key principles running through his work which we can deduce from his projects and from what he says about them. Three of these principles relate to art, urbanism, and ecology: he avoided symmetry; the proportions of projects mediate between the wider landscape and the human figure; and elements of the landscapes, such as plants, are understood in terms of their relationship to other elements.

The curves of the early work such as the Ministry of Education and Health and the Fazenda Marambaia with their wide planting beds became an oft-repeated feature in Burle Marx's projects. These curves rarely replicate themselves, giving a feeling of movement and vitality. Burle Marx's landscapes became more geometric later in life but they are essentially designed within the same parameters he established early in his career. These curves were typically marked with materials such as grass, water, concrete curbs (mostly cast in situ), and basalt setts. They were influenced by the work of other artists as well as the Brazilian landscape.

The proportions of the Copacabana Beachfront borrows from the surrounding landscape, and takes its proportions from it. So too does the Fazenda Marambaia, the Parque del Este, Flamengo Park, and the Fazenda Vargem Grande, where the mountains disappear with the dark of night and reappear in the morning light. The same could be said of most of Burle Marx's landscapes, except where the scheme is completely enclosed, or in a very flat site as in Brasília. The designed landscape becomes the inter-mediary between the intimate human scale and the wider landscape, the physical and the emotional. "Just as color is enriched by contrast with another color, so a plant assumes a new significance when placed beside another plant," he tells us in *Gardens and Ecology.* Burle Marx uses music to illustrate the relationship of plants to one another. In *The Garden as a Form of Art* he tells us, "One may think of a plant as a note. Played in one chord, it will sound in a particular way; in another chord, its value will be altered. Sometimes it is the keynote, sometimes a third related both up and down the scale; it can be legato, staccato, loud or soft, played on a tuba or on a violin. But it is the same note." Plants had for Burle Marx a spiritual significance, as Ono reported: "God is a kind of energy, a form of energy, and is in everything, in nature, in everything.…He thinks that God for him is a big power, is something big and he thinks it is everywhere; in the flower, the beginning of the flower, the bee that takes the pollen.…"[39] At the time of his death on June 4, 1994, Burle Marx was a national celebrity in Brazil and one of the best-known landscape architects in the world. He is buried under the shade of a mango tree in a cemetery in Guaratiba beside his "second mother," Anna Piascek.[40]

3.   Notes on the Lectures

In a lecture delivered at Harvard University, *Finding a Garden Style to meet Contemporary Needs* (note the term "garden"), the original typed manuscript begins, "It may seem strange to you that a landscape gardener from the tropics.…" [p. 178] Burle Marx firmly scored out "gardener," replacing it with "architect." [pp. 145–49] His successor as director of the studio, Haruyoshi Ono, affirmed that this was typical of Burle Marx, explaining that Burle Marx was very sensitive to being called a landscape gardener, rather than a landscape architect. Burle Marx cringed at this term, especially later in life: he considered it a discourtesy.[41]

Practice

Burle Marx practiced his landscape architecture mostly in Brazil, where to this day there is still little formal landscape architectural education: disciplinary training frequently comes through professional practice and is often self-taught, as it was for Burle Marx. Training for landscape architects is still mostly subsumed within schools of architecture and urbanism. Burle Marx's background in the arts placed him outside that particular professional coterie, unlike his mentors and contemporaries such as Niemeyer. In *The Landscape Architect in the World, Today,* Burle Marx calls for greater inclusion of landscape architecture within design education: "We feel that the teaching of these fundamental aspects should be emphasized in architecture and urbanism schools." [p. 230] It is notable that he did not call for new educational programs, but for reform of existing architecture and urbanism education to include more landscape architecture. We can deduce that Burle Marx supported the integration of design disciplines rather than their further separation, signaling his awareness of the breadth of skills needed to manage the ecological complexity of the design of the constructed environment. In doing so, he acknowledges the importance of the role of the architect and urbanist, a group from which he felt excluded. Clearly, by today's standards, Burle Marx's lack of formal education in landscape architecture would work against him, and may even preclude him from membership in professional institutes of landscape architecture internationally; yet, he was one of the most prolific and influential landscape architects of his day. In his lectures, as in his practice, Burle Marx challenged the professional boundaries and norms of landscape architecture. Burle Marx changed the center of landscape architecture by engaging from the peripheries; expanding and enriching the discipline.

In looking beyond professional limitations, toward the arts, urbanism, and ecology, Burle Marx succeeded in broadening the scope of the profession of landscape architecture and perceptions of it. Although highly honored for his contribution to landscape architecture worldwide, Burle Marx rarely studied the work of other landscape architects and avoided membership in professional institutes. At one stage, Roberto only had two landscape books–*Modern Gardens* by Sir Peter Shepheard and *Gardens in the Modern Landscape* by Christopher Tunnard.[42] Burle Marx admired the work of Lawrence Halprin and especially Luis Barragán. He knew little of Geoffrey Jellicoe's work but liked him as a person. His book collection developed

e   Parque del Este
Caracas, 1956
Plan. Gouache, 49⅛ × 38 in (124.8 × 96.5 cm)

f   Flamengo Park
     Rio de Janeiro, 1954–1964
     Perspective view, 1961. Drawing on paper vellum,
     27½ × 39 in (70 × 99 cm)

into a substantial library in later years, and one book, *Studies in Landscape Design Vol. 2* (still in the library of the Sítio) bears the inscription, "In appreciation of the evening of December 14th, 1967, and for your contribution to the art of landscape. Geoffrey Jellicoe."

Landscape

One might ask how Burle Marx practiced landscape architecture in a society not only where the profession did not formally exist, but also where there is barely a word for landscape, the nearest Portuguese equivalent being *paisagem,* meaning a "view."[43] Burle Marx's eagerness to be referred to as a landscape architect was no doubt hampered, at least in Brazil, by the lack of an adequate term in Portuguese for the profession, where the closest is *arquiteto paisagista,* an "architect of the view." He doesn't help the situation by constantly referring to gardens, *jardim,* in his lectures, albeit for want of a better term. Likewise, he uses "landscaping" again and again, derived from *paisagismo,* and the term translates in English to the actions of a landscaper. The multilingual Burle Marx was deeply aware of the problem with terminology, despite his recurrent use of "garden" and "landscaping."[44] Laurence Fleming points out an interesting cultural conundrum caused by this problem with terminology whereby the artist would be invited through the front door, but the gardener through the back door. People did not know what to do with Burle Marx![45]
Burle Marx tells us in *Finding a Garden Style to Meet Contemporary Needs* that his premise for landscape architecture is to mold the land for aesthetic and practical concerns: "If I were ever asked what the first philosophical assumption for my garden would be, I would immediately answer that it was the same attitude which reveals the conduct of Neolithic man: to transform the natural topography in order to adjust it to human needs, individual and collective, utilitarian and pleasing." [p. 89] Although he uses the term "garden" for want of a better Portuguese alternative, Burle Marx could be describing landscape in a broader sense. In *The Garden as a Form of Art,* he tells us that: "The art of garden design is a very—and perhaps the most—complex art, demanding an understanding of the other arts and a willingness to learn from nature." [p. 105] He also saw the practice of landscape architecture as a holistic practice that didn't end on the drawing board or with the project's construction. He acknowledged the role of maintenance: "Today, when labor is at a premium, when practically no one, even in Brazil, can afford a full-time gardener, when municipal gardeners are an infinitesimal proportion of city employees, the problem of upkeep as well as layout is a primary consideration," [p. 181] he tells us in *Finding a Garden Style to Meet Contemporary Needs.* Whatever Burle Marx's terminology, his work on gardens and landscapes encompasses a vision of the city and an ethical stance on art, ecology, complexity, function, nature, and social use.

Burle Marx saw it as incumbent upon the landscape architect to engage in seeking social and environmental justice. His many plant-hunting expeditions in the Brazilian interior exposed him firsthand to environmentally destructive practices that tragically persist to this day. He saw it as part of his duty as a landscape architect to challenge these unjustifiable practices. Throughout his life he protested against the wanton demolition of the Amazon rainforest and the eradication of native Brazilian flora from their habitats. In *The Garden as a Form of Art* he asserts, "It is for the landscape architect to try and prevent the destruction of the natural environment…." [p. 118] He capitalized on his celebrity in Brazil to campaign against the loss of indigenous flora in rural Brazil and the Amazon rainforest, through television and media interviews. In *Gardens and Landscape,* when speaking of the diversity of landscapes in Brazil, he informs us, "And I had to fight for its defense and survival." [p. 159] In the same lecture he declares that the work of the landscape architect goes beyond the aesthetic to ethical concerns. He tells us "that the mission of preserving the landscape […] goes beyond the work of composition. One must bring nature into the reach of man and, above all, take man back to nature." [p. 159] Burle Marx saw the landscape architect as someone who should be deeply engaged in landscape and environmental conservation as well as design.

Burle Marx's activism was not merely protest. He saw an expanded role for the landscape architect in civil society, in which the landscape architect is proactive in environmental conservation and applies this sensibility in designing new landscapes. Through fieldwork, he actively collected plants for conservation and also for use in his gardens. In this sense, Burle Marx's fieldwork was about action as well as discovery. In *The Function of the Garden,* he tells us: "It is our duty to respect what we have and perpetuate, by means of seed collections, nurseries, transplanting of seedlings, grafting, layering, etc., all this remaining flora that challenges us calls for a more intelligent utilization, so as to provide us with an aesthetic and ethical sense of existence." [p. 176] It is not surprising, therefore, that as already stated, Burle Marx's plant collection of native Brazilian plants amounted to more than 3,500 species. Haruyoshi Ono recalled that it was not uncommon for Burle Marx to use a particular plant in a landscape, judging it on its form, volume, and texture, and only later learn that it was named after him.[46]

Judging from the numbers of newspaper articles and press releases attributed to Burle Marx, he had a prolific engagement with the media. A single lecture at a U.S. university, or a public appearance by Burle Marx at one of his frequent exhibition openings, would lead to a flurry of articles, including local and national newspapers such as the *Ohio Star,* the *St. Louis Post,* and the *Philadelphia Inquirer,* which documented his 1993 visit to the opening of the Cascade Gardens at Longwood Gardens outside

Philadelphia. These articles shared similar content and clearly were based on the same press release. "I'm a plant eater!" he declared in a report in the *Tampa Tribune* on his 1986 lecture at the Harvard Graduate School of Design in Cambridge, Massachusetts (included in this volume as *Finding a Garden Style to Meet Contemporary Needs*).[47] Another carries the headline, "Landscape Expert Wants to Color Cities Green," reporting on a talk at the Missouri Botanical Garden, where he argued that green areas were essential for the tranquility and mental health of urban dwellers.[48] Studio Burle Marx had an effective publicity machine, which was an important aid to his activism.

Urbanism

The relationship of Burle Marx's work with the city is a central theme in his discourse, especially in his later lectures. He paints a picture of himself not just as a romantic botanist and artist but as an avowed urbanist who saw a distinct role for landscape architecture within the contemporary city. In *The Garden as a Form of Art,* Burle Marx acknowledges that it was not enough to garden: "The garden has left the hand of the gardener, who although he may have had great knowledge of plant material was not solving the problems of the gardens of the modern city." Clearly, Burle Marx was aspiring toward a form of landscape architecture which interacted with the contemporary city. In the same lecture he tells us, "The function of the landscape architect today is to make known the part a garden has to play in the cities of our lives." [p. 120]

Burle Marx's definition of a garden could be construed as an urban landscape, what he described as: "a careful selection of certain aspects of nature: water, rock, flower, and foliage; ordered and arranged by man; and in which man may have direct contact with plants. An area in space, however small, in which he may find rest, relaxation, recreation, and above all the feeling that he is living in, and integrated into, this space. It is also a complex of plastic intentions, with a utilitarian purpose: and it should, whenever possible, fuse with the surrounding landscape, while being an extension of the architecture for which it is designed." [p. 178]

In *The Function of the Garden,* Burle Marx links what he termed the "city garden" to the "urban question." Burle Marx sought to create beautiful spaces that also served a wider social purpose: "The city garden, whether it is a garden planned for a school, an industrial plant, or a hospital, assumes a greater significance because it is closely linked to the urban question." [p. 173] In the same lecture, he calls for the preservation of urban green areas, "allowing the city dweller contact with nature, and not leading him to feel lost in a mass of concrete that little by little takes possession of the scanty free space still left in large cities." [p. 173] Although Burle Marx sees a distinction between green areas and cities, his words might not seem as radical today because landscape architecture has come much closer to Burle Marx's point of view in the integration of matters of urbanism, landscape, ecology, art, and countryside.

It is in the understanding of the city as a landscape that Burle Marx's words offer most promise. He understands the elements a city gardener would design with to include more than green space and vegetation. "In New York, or even in Rio de Janeiro, the neon signs, the advertising posters, the traffic lights, the lighting of parkways–these are not problems that can be ignored. From these is born a new aesthetics," he states in the postscript to *The Garden as a Form of Art.* [p. 120] If Burle Marx were working today, one wonders how his play with new aesthetics, including colors, forms, sounds, textures, and volumes could be applied to the contemporary city, especially considering the huge scale and complexity of some landscape projects. Burle Marx perceived the aesthetic and ethical associations of large-scale infrastructure works and carved out a role for himself, and in doing so carved out a role for landscape architecture in projects such as Flamengo Park and Copacabana Beachfront. "The gardens of our grandfathers, the grottos, the pagodas, the ruins, all designed to evoke a past remembered with nostalgia, are not the matters of today," he asserts in *The Garden as a Form of Art.* [p. 120] In *The Landscape Architect in the World Today,* he refers to the landscape architect "as a creator and organizer of the urban space," [p. 225] ascribing to landscape architects–with their eye for color, form, and geometry–a role often associated with city planners. Imagine, for example, the potentials of approaching the design of a city with color as a starting point?

Burle Marx's work is not widely interpreted from the point of view of the urbanist. Anita Berrizbeitia's work on the Parque del Este in Caracas is a notable exception. Berrizbeitia points out not just the contemporaneity of Burle Marx's landscape architecture but also situates Burle Marx's Parque del Este within the cultural, political, and social situation in Caracas in the late 1950s and early 1960s. Notably, Berrizbeitia suggests that Burle Marx's work in Caracas was an inspiration for a whole generation of Venezuelan landscape architects, providing a middle ground between the European-inspired urban landscapes and the "raw tropical nature." [49]

Design for People

It is in his social agenda that Burle Marx's lectures are perhaps most surprising. In several lectures Burle Marx tells us that he is motivated by people, by the collective, and by society. While this is very much consistent with his role as an activist, the general perception of Burle Marx's landscape architecture was that he did not care about the client or user, but did his own thing. Sir Geoffrey Jellicoe put it bluntly, "You see, what he does is he will walk onto a site and do the swishing and do these lovely things,

g   Fazenda Vargem Grande, Garden of Volumes
Areias, SP, 1979
Pen and ink, 43 × 21 in (110 × 53.5 cm)

mind it will be his thing, it will be what he wants to have there and very nice, worthwhile it is too."[50] Even Haruyoshi Ono would confirm this approach: that Burle Marx did what he himself wanted, but that over time he began to consider the user more carefully. "In the beginning before I started to work with Roberto, he just said 'I think I want this garden' and made it. But then I started to work with him and tried to, more or less, open his mind and said 'you have to listen to the client because the garden is for the client.' Then he became more open for the client."[51]

In *Finding a Garden Style to Meet Contemporary Needs,* Burle Marx tells us that, "a work of art cannot be, I think, the result of a haphazard solution." [p. 189] He applied what he termed a series of principles–not formulas–to his projects. He claims in *Concepts in Landscape Composition,* to have "never deliberately sought originality as an aim." Having been initially trained as a painter–who works alone–Burle Marx brought the attitude of the "great maestro" to his landscape architecture, even though, through his firm, he provided full-service design, from concept to maintenance. Despite–or indeed because of–his concern for the users, and their quality of life and their needs, he believed very much in the agency of design. In *Gardens and Ecology,* he tells us, "The social mission of the landscape architect has a pedagogical side of communicating to the masses a feeling of esteem and comprehension of the values of nature through his presentation of it in parks and gardens." [p. 143] Burle Marx saw the potential of design to educate on the environment, in addition to the ability of changing the quality of lives through his landscape architecture.

Burle Marx's lectures show the social intentions of his artistry. In *Concepts in Landscape Composition,* he asserts that, "A garden has not only a decorative function; today it is above all aimed for the collective, and integrated into questions of town planning." [p. 97] In *The Garden as a Form of Art,* Burle Marx declares, "But if, in the course of each day, even one person will pause for a moment, and stand, and look, and feel renewed–then that piece of work will not have been in vain." [p. 119] In *The Garden as a Way of Life,* he tells us that "the purpose of the garden is to be a spatial condition of community life." [p. 124] In *The Landscape Architect in the World Today,* he argues that it is essential for the landscape architect, "the organizer of urban space," [p. 228] to better understand social relationships and argues for collaborative design teams that include economists and sociologists. He tells us, "It is also essential for the organizer of urban space to understand social structures and group tendencies; hence the importance of the participation of the sociologist and the economist in the staff, for programming and planning." [p. 228] The association of aesthetic, economic, and social dimensions of the urban landscape is essential for understanding Burle Marx's words and work.

Plural Ecologies

In *Gardens and Ecology,* Burle Marx describes a nighttime phenomenon he observed in the arid Caatinga biome in northeastern Brazil. He marvels at how the white flowers of the cardeiro cactus (*Cereus jamacaru*) opened gently in the moonlight, "offering their deep, white throats to thousands of insects." The careful choreography of the cactus flower and insects that descended upon them as soon as their flowers opened at dusk were a matter of delight and wonder for Burle Marx. The flowers of this cactus last only for one night and they wither before morning. He tells us that such compatibilities, whether they be plant-animal or plant-plant relationships, or even color-color, depend on a whole range of factors including the soil and climate, which are not accidental but "associations," the foundation for community ecology interactions which determine species persistence and the sustainability of community structure.[52] Burle Marx aspired to create associations in his work. One might imagine swarms of people flocking across Rio to Flamengo Park at dusk, just as the flies descend on the cactus flower. But such associations exist across scales from the very small plant and material groupings within a roof garden to the very large-scale urban projects like Flamengo Park. The urbanism exists in the complex relationships between the various parts from the small to the large.

Burle Marx certainly inspired movements toward more "ecological" and "urban" approaches in landscape architecture.[53] While many landscape architects of the same era of heightened environmental awareness became seduced by process over form, Burle Marx retained his focus on design. "He is required to construct an artifice," he demands of the landscape architect in *Concepts in Landscape Composition.* In *The Plant,* he remarks, "In landscape architecture one cannot possibly speak of aesthetics in any isolated way." For him, design was related to plants, materials, and people. It is in the relationships between the various facets of Burle Marx's work—activism, aesthetics, art, botany, conservation, ethics, music, sound, texture, the social, the urban—that make Burle Marx's landscape architecture so successful. His far-ranging associations created new ecologies—to use the term in a plural, Guattarian, sense.[54] He expanded the field of landscape architecture, embracing its multidisciplinary nature, and set an ideal that goes far beyond the normal confines of the discipline. Burle Marx's lectures demonstrate his mastery of botany, of art, of urbanism, of social and environmental ethics; and of the profession of landscape architecture in a way that is increasingly relevant, suggesting a model for contemporary landscape architectural practice. Burle Marx's words bring a radical perspective—and their application a "new aesthetics"—to the practice of landscape architecture and the shaping and reshaping of what he terms "the cities of our lives."

1   Sima Eliovson, *The Gardens of Roberto Burle Marx* (Portland, OR: Timber Press, 1991), 10.

2   Sir Geoffrey Jellicoe, in discussion with the author, January 1994.

3   Sir Peter Shepheard, in discussion with the author, July 1995.

4   A volume of Roberto Burle Marx's lectures was published in 1987 in Portuguese. See: *Arte e Paisagem: Conferências Escolhidas,* ed. José Tabacow (São Paulo: Nobel, 1987). A revised and expanded edition was published in 2004. Also, three of Burle Marx's lectures were published in English, in *Roberto Burle Marx: The Modernity of Landscape.* See *Roberto Burle Marx: The Modernity of Landscape,* eds. Laura Cavalcanti, Farès el-Dahdah, and Frances Rambert (Barcelona: Actar, 2011).

5   Eliovson, 21.

6   Portuguese, German, French, English, Spanish, Italian.

7   *Gartenschönheit* was a journal edited by gardeners Karl Foerster and Camillo Schneider, published in Berlin between 1920–1938, and then later as *Gartenbau im Reich* between 1941–1944.

8   William Howard Adams, *Roberto Burle Marx: The Unnatural Art of the Garden* (New York: Museum of Modern Art, 1991), 10.

9   Laurence Fleming, *Roberto Burle Marx: A Portrait* (Rio de Janeiro: Editora Index, 1996), 23.

10   John G. Stoddart, in discussion with the author, 1996.

11   Frederick Gregory, "Roberto Burle Marx: The One-Man Extravaganza," *Landscape Architecture* 71, no. 3 (1981): 367–47.

12   Conrad Hamerman, "Roberto Burle Marx: The Last Interview," *The Journal of Decorative and Propaganda Arts* 21 (1995): 164.

13   Ibid.

14   Ibid.

15   Fleming, 31.

16   Hamerman, 164.

17   Roberto Burle Marx in Fleming, 31.

18   Fleming, 34.

19   Gregori I. Warchavchik (1896–1972) was a Ukranian-Brazilian architect who had arrived in Brazil in the early 1920s.

20   Hamerman, 166.

21   Jane Holz Kay, "Plants are Landscape Architect's Palette," *Tampa Tribune,* September 6, 1986.

22   *Victoria regia* has been renamed *Victoria amazonica* after its native habitat.

23   Stoddart, 1996.

24   Haruyoshi Ono, in discussion with the author, 1996.

25   Riberio Dias, in discussion with the author, 1996.

26   Anita Berrizbeitia, *Roberto Burle Marx in Caracas: Parque del Este, 1956–1961* (Philadelphia: University of Pennsylvania Press, 2005).

27   Stoddart, 1996.

28   Geoffrey and Susan Jellicoe, *The Landscape of Man: Shaping the Environment from Prehistory to the Present Day* (New York: Viking Press, 1975), 324.

29   Fleming, 54.

30   Bruno Zevi, "The Modern Dimension of Landscape Architecture," *Journal of the Institute of Landscape Architects* 60 (1962): 18–19.

31   Hans Broos, in discussion with the author, 1996.

32   Haruyoshi Ono, in discussion with the author, 1996.

33   Flavia Quintanilha & Rodrigo Fernandes Architects pointed this out in an Instagram post, August 2017.

34   Fleming, 73.

35   Haruyoshi Ono, 1996.

36   Enrico Caruso (1873–1921) was an Italian opera tenor whose work was widely recorded.

37   See *Lost Paradise: The Gardens of Roberto Burle Marx,* BBC One, October 6, 1992.

38   Ibid.

39   Ibid.

40   Haruyoshi Ono, in discussion with the author, 2014. Ono said it was he, his wife, Fatima, and Burle Marx's personal assistant, Maria Amalia, who decided where Roberto be buried.

41   Ibid.

42   Stoddart, 1996.

43   There have been notable efforts to establish a landscape architecture profession in Brazil, as well as distinct educational programs, in recent years.

44   For more on the various identities of
       "landscape," see *Is Landscape…?
       Essays on the Identity of Landscape,*
       eds. Gareth Doherty and Charles
       Waldheim (Abbingdon, U.K.: Routledge,
       2015), as well as my essay, "In the west
       you have landscape, here we have…"
       *Studies in the History of Gardens and
       Designed Landscapes* 34, no. 3 (2014):
       201–6.
45   Fleming, 54.
46   Haruyoshi Ono, in discussion with the
       author, 1996.
47   Roberto Burle Marx in Kay, September 6,
       1986.
48   Charles Prost, "Landscape Expert
       Wants to Color Cities Green," *St. Louis
       Post-Dispatch,* May 16, 1983.
49   Berrizbeitia, 85.
50   Jellicoe, 1994.
51   Ono, 1996.
52   I am grateful to Steven Handel
       for bringing community ecology
       interactions to my attention.
53   See Ian McHarg's *Design with Nature*
       (New York: Wiley, 1969), and Anne
       Whiston Spirn's *The Garden: Urban
       Nature and Human Design* (New York:
       Basic Books, 1985), for instance, as
       well as later movements in landscape
       and ecological urbanism.
54   Writing around the same time as Burle
       Marx, the French social scientist
       Félix Guattari argued that the problem
       of the contemporary city, what one
       might call the "urban question," cannot
       be resolved with an environmental
       approach alone. Rather a more
       holistic approach is necessary, one
       that embraces what he called
       the three ecological registers of the
       environmental, mental, and social.
       See Félix Guattari, *The Three Ecologies,*
       trans. Ian Pindar and Paul Sutton
       (London: Athlone Press, 2000). Also
       Ecological Urbanism, eds. Mohsen
       Mostafavi and Gareth Doherty (Zurich:
       Lars Müller Publishers, 2016).

This book contains twelve lectures delivered by Roberto Burle Marx between 1954 and 1986 and not all dates were verified. Lectures 1–9 were gifted to me by Haruyoshi Ono in 1996. Lectures 10–12 were later located in Burle Marx's archive in Rio de Janeiro. Some of the lectures, such as Lecture 4, *Gardens and Ecology,* were delivered again and again over a long time span, with just minor variations in content. Others were radically changed between the original Portuguese and the English translations. Some lectures (Lectures 3, 5, and 8) appear to exist only in English. In one instance (Lecture 11), the English translation predates the published Portuguese version, in which case the English translation was used as the definitive source. For this reason, the lectures are not arranged chronologically, but in the approximate order in which they were archived.

These lectures were not written as individual chapters; each lecture is a unit unto itself. They were written to be performed, rather than read as a text. As a result, the argumentation mode can be a little scattered–traveling from history (often Burle Marx's personal version of history), into botany, and then back to history, on to design, etc. As is often the case with lectures, they naturally contain repetitions of ideas and facts (especially between Lectures 3 and 4) and these repetitions are by and large maintained in the text in the interest of respecting the autonomy of each lecture.

The lectures were delivered at many institutions and events internationally including Harvard University, the Massachusetts Institute of Technology, the University of Georgia, Iowa State University, and the annual conferences of the American Society of Landscape Architects (ASLA). The typical format for a lecture by Roberto Burle Marx was that he would lecture from these texts, and then follow his delivery with a slide show of his built work. All but two of the lectures that are reproduced here are a direct result of this format. According to Haruyoshi Ono, Burle Marx disliked the format often favored by designers of talking and showing slides at the same time. Indeed Burle Marx's lunchtime address to the ASLA Meeting in 1985 was not included in this volume for this very reason as he was mostly referring to slides, his lecture becoming more about the slides than ideas. Lecture 8, *Finding a Garden Style to Meet Contemporary Needs,* is an example of a lecture with annotations of slides integrated with the lecture (see insert on pages 145–49).

Many plant names are cited, more so than could be endnoted. Instead descriptions are added in parentheses where appropriate. Where plant names were given by Burle Marx in Latin, they follow the standard genus-species format, italicized and the genus capitalized (e.g., *Heliconia burle-marxii*). When only the genus is specified, it remains italicized and capitalized. Often in his lectures, Burle Marx would refer to plant kingdom family names; these terms are capitalized but not italicized, in accordance to the treatment of scientific terms by the Chicago Manual of Style. When the given common name is a term that doesn't have a corresponding standard English name, the Portuguese common name is italicized and in lowercase (e.g., *tinhorão*). When a plant is referred to by its common English-language name, it is in roman and lowercase, with the exception of a proper noun or adjective in its name which is capitalized (e.g., water lily, baobab tree, Australian Pine).

I am acutely aware of the unsuitability of lecture notes for publication in this format, and the myriad problems faced when trying to adapt a lecture into a coherent text. These texts were not written for publication, and many facts had to be checked and not all were verified in the process. To edit these texts too much would be to reduce Burle Marx's own voice, which is an important part of the experience of this book. Not to edit at all would be to perpetuate some of the mistakes in the text and differences in language and emphasis that have taken place in the last fifty years.

Burle Marx often capitalized the "n" in "Nature." These texts were written at a time when ideas of pristine and "natural" nature were embedded in public discourse. One thinks of Ian McHarg's *Design with Nature* and Rachel Carson's *Silent Spring,* and might sadly recognize there is little of untouched nature left. Descriptions of humankind as "man," as was common in his time, have been retained; references to "Indians" have been changed to Amerindians; and a few other references which were not intended to be offensive but which might be considered offensive today have been removed. Burle Marx's delightful use of the third person when talking about himself has been retained, as have made-up words such as "velloziform." In line with Burle Marx's own preferences, when not explicitly discussing a garden, the term "gardener" or "landscape gardener" has been changed to "landscape architect." Likewise, the word "landscaper" has almost always been changed to reflect the work he actually did rather than a literal translation of the word he used. The lectures are balanced between the desire to keep faith with the originals and adapting them to make them more applicable to the present day. Significant changes—usually longer than a phrase or a sentence—are indicated with endnotes. Changes of one sentence or less are generally not noted. Significant phrases are highlighted in the book with a larger font and these emphases relate purely to ideas rather than syntax or intonation.

Lastly, the lectures were written for speaking, for performance in front of an audience. Therefore, they make more sense when heard as spoken words rather than read silently. To overcome this disorientation in the formatting, I ask you to join me in reading the lectures out loud. In doing so, allow Burle Marx's words, overflowing with energy, ideas, and opinions fill the room in the same way as they fill the page. Imagine Roberto "like a peppercorn," as one of his friends once described him, "very hot, and very strong," and occasionally getting up your nose.

Concepts in Landscape Composition

Original lecture in Portuguese dating from 1954. The English translations from Burle Marx's archive contain an extended ending which is included as a postscript. There are three English versions dating from 1970, one with Burle Marx's handwritten annotations on the typed script; another without annotations (but missing the first page); and also one revision by an unnamed editor, dated 1973.

The experience I have achieved through my work as a landscape architect, building and maintaining gardens, parks, and large town areas since virtually the third decade of the 20th century, allows me now to express my concept of the garden problem as an application of adequate knowledge of the ecological environment to meet the requirements of civilization.[1]

This concept–I mean my present idea, based on personal experience–claims no originality, no discovery; especially because my work responds to my own biographical path and to consideration of the natural environment.

In connection with my life as an artist, from the most rigorous disciplinary training in drawing and painting, my landscape architecture career is in fact the result of a series of accidental circumstances.[2] My interest was always in adapting to nature itself the fundamentals of composition according to the aesthetic feelings of our time.[3] In short, it was my method of organizing and composing my drawing and my painting, using less conventional materials.

I can largely explain my approach to art in terms of what happened to my generation when the artists were stricken by the impact of Cubism and abstraction. The juxtaposition of the plastic attributes of those aesthetic movements with natural elements created the attraction to a new experience. I decided to use natural topography as a surface for composition and the elements of nature, mineral and vegetable, as materials for the plastic organization, the very thing which other artists try to do on canvas with paint and brush.

The critics who are most interested in my work have repeatedly pointed out the stylistic connection between my painting and my landscape architecture. Geraldo Ferraz and Clarival Valladares have considered all my work as developing from a single flexible unit,[4] and I am the first to agree that there are no aesthetic differences between the object of painting and the object of constructed landscapes. Only the means of expression differ.

With the passing of time, as my experience grew further with nature and the work destined to it, I gradually formed a better awareness

of the work I was developing. I am not here to judge my work, but
to help toward the understanding of it, of its logic and functions within
its place and time.[5]

I insistently refuse to recognize the most frequent and common
judgment that is usually made of my work, pointed out as originality.
I have never deliberately sought originality as an aim.[6]

My philosophical concept of constructed landscape–I mean gardens,
parks, or developed town areas–is based on the historical direction
of all eras, recognizing in each period the expression of the aesthetic
thinking that is manifested in the other arts. In this sense, my work
reflects modernity, the date on which it takes place, but never loses
sight of the reasons for its own tradition, which are valid and
necessary.

If I were ever asked what the first philosophical assumption for
my garden would be, I would immediately answer that it was the same
attitude which reveals the conduct of Neolithic man: to transform
the natural topography in order to adjust it to human needs, individual
and collective, utilitarian and pleasing. There are two landscapes: the
untouched and the human-touched, constructed landscape.[7] The
latter corresponds to all interferences imposed by necessity. However,
beyond those necessities satisfying economic demand (transport,
supply, cultivation, housing, manufacturing industry, etc.), we can find
also the landscape determined by aesthetic need, which means
no luxury or waste, but an absolute need for human life, without which
civilization itself would lose its ethical purpose. To build a garden
means to act ethically and aesthetically.[8]

In different regions, there are periods when social equilibrium
determines artificial landscape configuration. It is no exaggeration to
affirm that the history of the garden (I mean constructed landscape)
is related to the history of the ethical and aesthetic ideals of the
corresponding age.

It is true that the West has a different landscape history from the
East. Different and poorer, and also more recent. On the other hand,
it is well known to what extent Western landscape has owed a debt to
Eastern influence since the 14th century in Italy, and even earlier on
the Iberian Peninsula.

If we want to mention in more remote history the presence of conceptual gardening, it is possible for us to refer to all periods, as early as examples of Neolithic behavior, that is, beginning with the first period of civilization when we can characterize sedentary behavior, agricultural activity, and utility-guided development in the applied arts (housebuilding, defense, and pottery).

The shape of vases and other utensils of Neolithic periods, as well as their decorative elements, reveals the presence of and the partiality for biomorphic themes: that means, for vegetable and animal elements of the surrounding nature, which partake of a certain degree of aesthetic reality.

This is why objects take on forms of natural patterns, which are already connected with human perception, emotion transfused with a sense of beauty having been added to the previously existing sense of utility.

Most of the examples of stylization of figures—vegetable and animal—from Neolithic behavior show us an attitude of contemplation, and, above this attitude, an artistic awareness, which determines the representation of the object out of its physical reality, sometimes transformed into symbols, but always presented in terms of plastic organization.

Once civilization is organized in clearer social and political structures (Egypt and Mesopotamia), the influence of artistic creation on the topographic natural landscape becomes more apparent. This is when architecture undertakes the task of bringing human thought and craving to bear upon the surroundings of physical nature, trying to alter its original shape to transform it into a vision of human dominion. The emergence of civilization is characterized not merely by a first recording of episode and code, but chiefly by conscious interference with the physical landscape to such a degree that it becomes possible to transform it into a man-made landscape, one able to establish the impact of the vision of ethical concepts (religious and political) and aesthetic concepts (preference of form, definition of noble materials, creation of styles) contained in the culture of each community.

Architecture and man-made landscape alike derive their structure from the ecological milieu. The natural conditions in the ancient Near

East should correspond with the choice of materials and the preferred solution to the artistic work.[9]

The mythology of such civilizations is frequently linked up with a landscape idea directly, or with the description of a built-up garden.[10]

The four daughters of Hesperus–the Hesperides–were gardeners of an orchard of golden apples, guarded by a dragon who never sleeps. In the Valley of Kings in Ancient Egypt, we can find a tomb inscription of a gardener of the pharaohs.[11]

The background of Hellenic mythology is a setting of dreamlike gardens and elements of botanical nature. The ornament of the Corinthian columns, the acanthus leaf and its legendary origin, shows us the aesthetic interaction between man and his natural environment, adopted as a suggestion for architectural development.[12] The whole meaning of the Dionysian myth (Bacchus) or the fable of Artemis (Diana), or of Aphrodite (Venus), involves ideas of a world of landscapes. The emergence of such early empires as the Chaldean-Assyrian civilization and Babylon points to fantastic gardens that already display a certain degree of ostentation and stateliness. It is proper here to note the legendary example of the Hanging Gardens of Babylon as an integration of constructed garden and architecture.

The different civilizations of western Asia (including Iran, Iraq, and the Mediterranean coast of Syria) are remembered in connection with episodes and constructions in the domain of landscape. The Sumerians, Babylonians, Chaldeans, Hittites, Hebrews, Assyrians, Persians, and all the other peoples of that area brought human history into the field of landscape architecture. Mesopotamia, between the Tigris and Euphrates, through its natural fertility, was woven into the legend of being the cradle of mankind and the original location of Eden, the paradise of Adam and Eve.

To mention only one of the ancestors of today's Western civilization, the Hebrew tradition, it is interesting to emphasize that Genesis as described in the Holy Bible evolves within a completely landscaped environment. God, creator of world and life, is, according to the Hebrew text, the builder, the artist of a landscape world, which He gave to man as a paradise in the form of a garden and orchard. The expulsion of Adam and Eve from this garden exposed them forever to vicissitudes and permanent suffering. There remained only as an ideal, the memory, the dream, the vision of a lost landscape. The loss of paradise engendered a feeling of everlasting frustration, and it thus became the role of the visual arts to recall it by means of invention. In the Christian era, when history reaches the Middle Ages and the early Renaissance, we can find in religious paintings the vision of a landscape, of a garden indicated as the lost paradise.

And when the Renaissance consolidates into a broad base of well-established elites differentiated in both their aesthetic customs and exigencies, then the great examples of constructed landscape emerge: a concept based on a close integration between architecture and topography.[13] The Renaissance garden is governed by a demand of plastic composition, of architectural treatment, and of absolute contention of forms and proposed dimensions.

Then comes the French garden, that is, the garden and the built landscape, which expresses the tastes of the nobility and the absolute power of the kings of France, with geometric solutions, with artifices (fountains, cascades, waterspouts, sculptures, etc.), but determined under a new plastic concern: that of spatial treatment, that is to say, the use of space as an element of construction, in order to convey the dazzle, the imposition of majesty.

Each following stylistic period is reflected, in one form or another, in its gardens. This correspondence has always occurred throughout history up to the present time.

The history of gardening and organized landscape in Brazil may be summed up in the following way:

From the first report of the discovery till the implantation of the empire in the beginning of the 19th century, we record the predominance of wild landscape, and only rare examples of built-up landscapes. Such are the town plans of Recife and Olinda, made by the Dutch in the first half of the 17th century under Prince Mauritius of Orange, and the gardens (gardened parks) of the late 18th century in Rio de Janeiro, beginning in 1753, when Rio became the capital of Brazil.

Brazilian sociologists, including Gilberto Freyre, show us a garden tradition starting from the patterns of rural civilization of sugar plantation in the old sugar mills of the states of Pernambuco, Alagoas,

Paraíba, Sergipe, and Bahia. They explain the architectural unit of house-chapel-mill, enlarged by the beautifying landscape treatment given to the orchard, with decorative plants used sometimes in the interest of giving a note of refined taste to the property itself. In Brazilian religious architecture from the first three centuries (since Brazil's founding), there are examples of the inner courtyards of convents and monasteries, where decorative plants were cultivated in removable vases, and used to beautify the church on feast days.

We also know, through sketches and engravings from visiting artists, of rural and town areas treated with a certain regularity of gardening, or, at least, showing the configuration of a composition and choice of elements. But, for the time being, these are insufficient examples and without definitive documentation, since we can find a great diversity among the sketches of different authors. Yet we cannot characterize a traditional Brazilian garden, either from the town-planning point of view or as an element of private life. We may, on the other hand, remember in the first phase, through all the long colonial period (16th–18th centuries), the beautifying artificial landscape of private, rural, and urban life, of orchards, of imported fruit trees (mango, avocado, sapodilla, lemon, etc.), and the production of chickens and domestic animals. From this custom, solutions known as "backyard," "farm," and "clearing," formed in Brazil,[14] corresponding to small and medium areas of private property, even those located in town areas.

In the case of farming, the most definitive peculiarity of the Brazilian rural phenomenon is the use of burned-over land for preparing the area for plantation. Very soon, more or less all over the country, the idea of wild nature was formed, an exuberant nature, superabundant, to be occupied for the utilization of the land. Nevertheless, sections of wild forest have always been preserved from destruction, sometimes as a necessity for the water supply in order to turn the mills, and sometimes, ludicrously, as a game reserve. The enormous geographical size of Brazil (3.3 million square miles or 8.5 million square kilometers), with the predominant population concentration in the cities and diluted in the countryside, justifies the diversity and the dispersion of the built-up landscape.

In the early 19th century the emperor of Portugal and Brazil, eager to develop the Brazilian Empire on the model of European civilizations, decided to introduce a series of modifications in its cultural characteristics. First, he ordered the opening of the ports, allowing the universalization of the country; second, he established the French Artist Mission and enlisted the aid of numerous group of scientists and professors to come to Brazil;[15] and finally, when he himself, Dom João VI (1767–1826), settled in Brazil, he assumed the initiative for various cultural enterprises. He created engineering schools, encouraged instruction in the arts and interest in the study of local nature, starting with the fantastic Botanical Garden (fantastic in his day) and various naturalist expeditions.[16]

Naturalistic knowledge of the land begins with Dom João VI; until his time, it was only studied in the Dutch period (1600–1625). It came to fruition in the works of Caspar Barlaeus, Willem Piso, and Georg Marcgrave and was documented in the painting and sketches of Frans Post, Albert Eckhout, and Zacharias Wagner.

The imperial court, the French Artist Mission, and the visiting naturalists of the 19th century (Carl Friedrich Philipp von Martius, Johann Baptist von Spix, Alexander von Humboldt, Augustin Saint-Hilaire, George Gardner, and others) have been the elements behind the complete modification of constructed landscape.[17] Numerous wild plants were selected for cultivation and passed into private decorative use. Many others of Asian, Antillean, African, and other origins were imported with immediate acclimatizing success. Agriculture, greatly enriched by immigration and through the coffee plantations (São Paulo, the Rio de Janeiro state) has formed a new element of interference in landscape.

In the period of the court and at the time of the Brazilian Empire (1822–1882), we record an excellent development in civil and private construction, and we may single out the work of Auguste-Henri-Victor Grandjean de Montigny, in Rio de Janeiro, of Louis-Léger Vauthier in Recife, and of the landscape architect Auguste François Marie Glaziou, author of the park of the imperial mansion (Quinta da Boa Vista) and the Campo de Santana in Rio de Janeiro.

The late half of the 19th century was characterized by work of an academic European character, preoccupied in showing mutual relationships with civilized centers and exhibiting the wealth of the recent nobility. With the fall of the Brazilian Empire, related to the abolition of slavery and the following economic crisis, a period of rearrangement of fortunes took place, which soon settled in the southern states, thanks to immigrant workers. This period, from 1880 to 1920, is marked by wealth and loss in the exploitation of Amazon rubber, by the industrialization of sugar, by the development of agriculture and cattle breeding, and by the great importation of European materials and goods. There appeared an elite bourgeois group, avid for status and civilized habits that would have to be manifested as a copy of European standards and customs, more in consumption than properly in artistic production. We can find in this time a great development with an extraordinary number of constructions for private and collective use in the principal cities (Rio de Janeiro, São Paulo, Salvador, Recife, Porto Alegre, and others) using European workers and craftsmen (immigrants from Portugal, Germany, Italy, and other countries) fixed in new patterns, characterizing the European contemporariness of the period and style called Art Nouveau. In Brazil it became better known as "floral style" in order to indicate the predominant sensibility, or an eclectic style denominated by irony, which people called "wedding cake."

There is an undeniable infatuation with the Belle Époque[18] and decadent European romanticism, but it is necessary to remember the excessiveness which took place in Brazil, to such degree that it nearly ruined our artistic and historic development, including religious artworks and ancient palaces, all made because of an extravagance of the newly rich with their anxiety for a civilization. From this period on, the Victorian influence, the taste for gardening and cultivation of flowers and exotic plants, becomes manifest in Brazil. The rose ruled in all arts, from poetry to the stucco in every house. Silver ferns,[19] Chinese bamboo, little palms in vases, carnations, chrysanthemums, dahlias, exotic ferns, etc., modeled botanical taste with decorative finality. This mighty remnant of the romanticism of the Belle Époque persisted in Brazil until the fourth decade of the 20th century.

This was the legacy, the collection of the artistic experience that I personally encountered when, back from Germany, I set out to be a simple plastic artist of my generation, in my land. For this reason, when I was asked when I perceived the aesthetic qualities of the native elements of the Brazilian flora, where I made the decision to build with the native flora an entire order of new plastic composition, for drawing, for painting, even reaching the landscape and the garden, which are the best-known part of my creation; I sincerely answer that it was as a student of painting, standing before a greenhouse of Brazilian tropical plants, in the Berlin-Dahlem Botanical Garden. Yes, it was there and then that I saw the force of genuine tropical nature, ready and in my hands, for the intention that it brought, then little defined, as suitable material for the plastic work that I looked to do. Since then I have used the genuine element of nature in all its strength and quality as material, organized in terms and purposes of a plastic composition. At least this is how I understand landscape architecture as a form of artistic expression.[20]

Postscript to English Translation

There existed at the same time as my personal revelation the gardens of Glaziou in the English style, in the middle of the 19th century and the "bungalows" and their gardens, of north American origin, whose basic ideas were published in Brazil through magazines like *House and Garden* and *House Beautiful,* and the French academic gardens in Paris Square (Praça Paris) in Rio de Janeiro.

The visits I made assiduously to the Berlin-Dahlem Botanical Garden, when I was studying there from 1928 to 1929, have been of fundamental importance in my creative intellectual development, through the paradoxical discovery of the Brazilian flora and of the ecological groupings created by Adolf Engler.[21]

It was this experience, and the impact made by my return to Brazil and my seeing again the academic and spurious gardens, in conflict with the surrounding landscape, that induced me to create gardens which are harmonious with the milieu, by examining how the artist reflects it, consciously or unconsciously. And it is in this sequence of ideas that we have to consider art, as a nonseparated phenomenon, as a diversity of manifestations which form a unit. The intimacy I had with botanists taught me to see plants better; my life in connection with arts in general taught me the importance of the transpositional element.

This is mainly the principle of transposition in arts, the element that helps one to a better understanding of the garden, where, among others, **the difference between pigment color and light color is fundamental.** Even though in gardens color is not used pictorially, we may speak of "garden color," definite or vague, intensified by light in transparency and textures propitiated by the counter-light and through the modulation of forms and volumes by solar and lunar light. This is why the possibilities of expression in gardens are so numerous: they are differentiated further through use of volumes, through planes, through borders, through the enlargement and the clearness of color, thanks to intermediary nuances and colorful surfaces.

A plant offers also a sculptural and arabesque aspect in its connection with other materials like stone, water, and sand. These elements of composition give a solid appearance and multiply the profiles of the plant. Wind also acts in the composition and the expectation of flourishing is a part of it. In the same way it is the movement and rustle of the water and the whisper of the leaves. **In all this context, it is important not to lose sight of the fact that plants live in interdependence of one another.**

We may speak also of the artistic principles which determine the field: **repetition, rhythm, surprise.** In this sense it is authentic to compare the language of the garden with musical language: there are prestos, andantes, fermatas, major, and minor. But in the sequences of tensions we cannot lose the connections among elements, just as in the structure of a symphony. I believe that the ideal consists in saying the maximum with a coherent and structured minimum.

A garden depends on the surrounding landscape, and it must be integrated to it and live in function with the people to whom it is destined. A garden has not only a decorative function; today it is, above all, aimed for the collective, and integrated into questions of town planning. It is necessary to carry the natural landscape into the garden by means of the local flora, to facilitate the social and pedagogical function of the garden, including helping people to discover the natural wealth in which they live.

The essence of the garden is its construction itself and the raw material–the plant–knowledge of whose cyclic behavior is indispensable, since the resultant forms of the manipulation of the constituent materials are inherent to the peculiar expression which we try to attain.

In this sense, I wish to give a contribution to the art which I have chosen, making good use of a flora not much used before me. I wish my gardens to have the refinements of the Japanese garden, where we can appreciate the shade of a flourishing cherry tree, projected onto the white sand or in moonlight.

I finish here with a word of praise to the element of the inexplicable, which allows us to create free of formulas, which has basis of impulse and improvisation, valid only in proportion to their submission to control, in proportion to the discipline of the artist himself.[22]

Text used for comparing the translation: Roberto Burle Marx, "Conceitos de composição em Paisagismo," in *Arte e Paisagem: Conferências Escolhidas,* ed. José Tabacow (São Paulo: Nobel, 1987), 11–18.

1   Original:…*às exigências naturais da civilização.*

2   Original:…*foi, de fato, uma sedimentação de circunstâncias.*

3   Original:…*os fundamentos da composição plástica.*

4   Geraldo Ferraz and Clarival Valladares were Brazilian journalists contemporary with Burle Marx.

5   Original:…*em suas razões e em sua função, para o meio e a época.*

6   Original: *Nunca a originalidade me preocupou como qualidade ou finalidade.*

7   Original:…*a natural, existente e a humanizada, construída.* Building on Cicero's idea of the second nature, a functional landscape, as opposed to primal wilderness, John Dixon Hunt reminds us that Renaissance humanists, such as Jacopo Bonfadio, regarded more refined landscapes as a "third nature." John Dixon Hunt, *Gardens and the Picturesque* (Cambridge: MIT Press, 1992), 3–4. Also see "Is Landscape Literature?" in *Is Landscape…? Essays on the Identity of Landscape,* eds. Gareth Doherty and Charles Waldheim (Abbingdon, U.K.: Routledge, 2015), 13.

8   "To build a garden means to act ethically and aesthetically," is present in the English translation but absent from the Portuguese edition.

9   Original: *As condições físicas do antigo Oriente Próximo haveriam de corresponder aos materiais escolhidos.*

10   Original:…*uma ideia paisagística.*

11   Probably referring to the tomb of Nakh, chief gardener from the Temple of Amun at Karnak. The gardens of the temple included kitchen gardens and a botanical garden.

12   Original:…*motivação da arquitetura.*

13   Original:…*paisagem artificial…*

14   Original:…*"quintal," "sítio,"* e *"roça."*

15   "…second, he established the French Artist Mission and enlisted the aid of numerous group of scientists and professors to come to Brazil" is present in the English translation but absent from the Portuguese edition.

16   "…and various naturalist expeditions" is present in the English translation but absent from the Portuguese edition.

17   The English translation also included references to "Harty, Derby, Eve-Lallemand" but they are omitted here and in the Portuguese edition.

18   Original: *correspondência.*

19   Original: *avenca,* "maidenhair fern."

20   This paragraph is present in the Portuguese edition but absent from the English translation.

21   Adolf Engler (1844–1930) was a German botanist.

22   "There existed at the same time as my personal revelation the gardens of Glaziou in the English style…in proportion to the discipline of the artist himself." This sentence is present in the English translation but absent from the Portuguese edition.

The Garden as a Form of Art

Original lecture in Portuguese dating from 1962. This text incorporates two undated versions of English translations, an abbreviated version, *The Garden as an Art in Living,* marked "obsolete," and *The Garden as a Form of Art,* most likely from a later date. A later version of this lecture, *The Garden as an Expression of Art,* was delivered at the Museum of Modern Art in New York on May 21, 1991.

The planned garden seems to have existed as long as written history; it is one of the oldest forms of art. In literature and mythology, it appears early as a conception of the ideal, as a dwelling place for gods–the Garden of Eden, the Garden of the Hesperides, the Garden of Allah.

We do not learn very much in detail about these gardens; it would be quite impossible to reconstruct the Garden of Eden from any specifications that occur in Genesis. But we can deduce, rather than discover, what they were supposed to be like; and they appear to have had one element in common. They are ordered reconstructions of nature herself, natural environments from which the element of fear has been removed and which grow in a most perfect and agreeable way with the laboring assistance of man. Where they occur, the objects to be feared are animal, or reptilian, and this to me seems to show that the garden in its ideal conception is a place where man can demonstrate his control of nature–if you like, his friendship for her–by acknowledging his dependence on her.

The garden is not simply a product of idle leisure, not merely one more way in which a successful egotist can add to his self-esteem. It is not a thing to be considered last when the money for a project has already been spent;[1] not a magic blanket to be flung over bad proportions or conflicting masses or poorly planned volumes. The garden is, it must be, an integral part of civilized life: a deeply felt, deeply rooted, spiritual, and emotional necessity.

The earliest gardens were derived inevitably from the immediate surroundings. Their function was to support and to preserve life. Even today, in the Amazon forests and in the thick scrubland of Mato Grosso this pattern exists.[2] Amerindians will settle for a time, they will plant maize and vegetables, and in the forest they will find medicinal and magic plants, stimulants (such as guarana),[3] fruits, and roots. But their lack of cultivation techniques and the habit of burning the soil for clearing force them eventually to move on. Early success in settled cultivation depended very much on gods and goddesses of fertility.[4] Today in Spanish-speaking America the help of San Isidro–*San Isidro, labrador, quita el agua y pon el sol*[5]–is always asked for; and even in

Protestant countries the knowledgeable and puritan inhabitants sometimes ask a blessing on the seed before it is planted.[6] But the old function of God and the gods belongs more and more to the agronomist and to the chemist:[7] with their help the role of the present-day horticulturalist tends to be to cultivate plants in places where they could not possibly grow naturally. We should not forget the humility of the early garden makers: their gardens both developed from the surrounding vegetation and depended on it.

With settlement came enclosure, protection against encroaching nature, defense against a hostile neighbor; and this has remained a constant feature in the history of garden design. Only in today's United States does the truly unenclosed garden exist, in the communal landscapes of the wealthy suburbs; a legacy, perhaps from the early settlers, who did not choose to provide the bushes for their enemies to hide in.[8] The English landscape garden of the 18th century, though apparently part of the landscape, was protected by distance from its neighbors, and by a ha ha, a sunken fence serving as a barrier to cows and sheep. Spiritually, these gardens were a sanctuary, sheltered from the wind, giving shade from the sun and relief from thirst and hunger. Architecturally, they were rooms without roofs, an extension of the house. Even the Hanging Gardens of Babylon, made to represent a mountain, had a square ground plan and were purely architectural in construction, though they were apart from the living quarters and intended to be viewed from afar. The design of a garden at Thebes, in Egypt, about 1400 B.C., is walled and purely rectilinear. It contains four ponds in two rectangular-shaped pairs, conveniently placed for watering the garden, and trees and palms in rows and blocks; and vines trained over pergolas. But the design is most elegant and the balance delicate, most carefully considered. It is not purely symmetrical as the house is not centrally placed–it is not even in the middle of one wall.[9]

Probably the plants used in these gardens were for use; but, brought this close to the house they inevitably offered an object for leisurely study. Gradually they came to be planted also for their beauty; and they came to supply forms to architecture–the lotus flower notably, and the acanthus leaf–to painting, sculpture, and to embroidery.

The Greeks produced the first public garden as we understand it. They were a gregarious people, with a strong community sense, fond of talking. From talking in the streets, they moved to the marketplace, and from there began to make gardens in which to talk. These had their origins in a sacred grove, dedicated either to a god or to a hero;[10] in the case of the Academy, it was to a hero, Academus, and in his honor games were played. The games required practice, so people came to train in the grove. This provided something to look at, so seats were supplied for the spectators. Covered walks, buildings, and baths followed, then statues to the winners of the games, and this produced a kind of garden–still essentially being made today–based on the needs of a society, adapted to urban surroundings and the landscape, in a gentle, unhurried, reasoned development, the function producing the aesthetic pattern.[11]

The Romans were better gardeners than the Greeks, and their natural conditions were more favorable. It is noticeable that the Roman goddesses Flora and Pomona had no counterparts in Greece.[12] They used the features of the Greek gardens, the grove, the pool, the colonnade, adapting them to urban gardens of the inward-looking, enclosed kind. Here the garden was often painted on a wall,[13] or merely suggested by a pergola; and lack of space also produced the roof garden, of which there is some evidence at Pompeii.[14] Then they evolved a country garden which, while basically an extension of the house, included a view of the landscape. It remained a sanctuary garden but, unlike the gardens of Islam, which, as one can still see today in Spain, turned their backs on the landscape, rejecting it utterly, the landscape was here acknowledged as a thing of beauty and recognized as an objective in its own right.

The garden of Pliny the Younger at Laurentum was chiefly planted with figs and mulberries, and the planted terraces took account of the view of the sea. He similarly refers to the view from another villa, in Tuscany, as being like "an imaginary landscape, made by a first-class artist," and he mentions the bushes of yew and boxwood carved into different shapes, which had now taken the place of statues in the Greek garden.[15] It was this type of garden that the beginning of the Renaissance would discover and that serves as a starting point for the planned gardens of our Western civilization.

The materials of a garden do not vary—water, stone, grass, trees and shrubs, flowers, and architectural features. It is their proportion, their relationship to one another that creates the differences in style. It is in the use of light, the use of textures, the understanding of a structure of a garden, and in the understanding of the plants which are to grow in it, that the artist expresses his thoughts. One must find a balance. The art of garden design is a very—and perhaps the most—complex art, demanding an understanding of the other arts and a willingness to learn from nature.[16]

In every art there is need for order, but not the kind of conventional order that can be imposed, like martial law. It must come from below; it must be the base on which one builds. One must select, blend, contrast, and complement, emphasize where necessary.

A garden should be, in short, a work of art—like painting, sculpture, tapestry, or a symphony.

Initially, the garden was called into existence for social reasons. There have been gardens made to be alone in, gardens to be together in, gardens to be alive in, and gardens to be dead in. There are gardens to impress one's friends (or to annoy one's enemies), gardens which include or exclude the landscape. While we should never lose sight of this initial function, we should never allow ourselves to be blinded by it; **for a thing which only proclaims and fulfills its function can never be a work of art.**[17]

The basis of all criticism must be an understanding of the artist's intention. That is how we must come to the study of the gardens of the past. It is possible today to walk through the woods of Versailles or the forest at Saint-Germain-en-Laye, and feel nothing but an overpowering melancholy. Today these gardens induce in us a mood of dreaming. But when we link our thoughts to the functions of the time for which they were created, when we populate them with huntsmen, brilliantly attired and mounted, the spectators bejeweled and plumed, glowing in silk and satin, then the melancholy leaves us and the tall avenues and dark glades revert in the mind's eye to their original purpose. Dutch paintings and engravings of gardens in the 17th century, especially, always have human figures in them. From them we can deduce that they were made for people to walk in, to talk in, and the figures, so to speak, were an integral part of the design.[18] It was the 19th century that excluded people from the designed garden, providing not only fixed objects of admiration but also fixed points from which to admire them; and this tendency has not altogether disappeared.

The garden has always been a part of the art of living. The Romans understood superbly the pleasures of living connected with the different functions of the garden: the vistas, shady walks and cool fountains, the aviary, the ornamental pond, which also supplied fish for the table, the swimming pool, and tepidarium.[19]

The gardens of Leon Battista Alberti, a Venetian who worked principally in Florence, were essentially places of leisure and rest. It appears to have been Alberti who, in about 1450, first tried to re-create the gardens of Pliny the Younger. "There should be," he says, "an aura of good-humored welcome."[20] The garden was conceived as an integral part of the house, not simply as an extension of it. It shared in creating the mood, which the intelligent person required for his home.[21] The house was to be set on a slight elevation, to obtain a fine view, but the ascent was to be gentle, effortless. Dark shadows were to be used in contrast with light. Above all, the main lines of the garden were to be kept "in strict proportion and regularity so that the pleasing harmony of the whole would not be lost in the attraction of the individual parts."[22]

It was necessary to say this; possibly, it is still so. The medieval garden, which Alberti inherited, was essentially a sanctuary garden for growing fruit, vegetables, and herbs. It was basically a square, sub-divided into other squares, neatly edged, the paths covered with pergolas. It was likely to contain plants in pots, an aviary, a balustraded fish pond, a pond for watering, an artificial hill, roses and honeysuckle, walls covered with fruit trees. From its interior, it was difficult to see more than one section of the garden at a time. It was designed to be looked at from above, from a castle wall or a high window. It was complex, but it was not chaotic. Alberti may be said to have imposed a Roman form on many of these features, adding statues and topiary; adopting the circle and the semicircle as shapes for planting; and introducing running water.

His gardens seem to have been—for they no longer exist—quiet and spacious. Alberti has a great deal to say about proportion. His gardens contain all the features that at one time or another were to dominate in the designed gardens of Europe. Sometimes it was to be flower beds, neatly arranged, and flower pots; sometimes the straight walk edged with trees; sometimes the roses and honeysuckle; sometimes the statues and the running water. But in the gardens of Alberti—if he obeyed his own precepts—one feels there might have been an interesting balance.

At the same time, in the Kingdom of Naples, whose kings were Spanish in origin, a type of garden based on the use of running water was developing. Around this time, Spain had been under Moorish rule for nearly eight hundred years, and Moorish gardens were built around water, which, according to Islamic religious precept, should always be in motion. The Spaniards who came to the court of Naples, and later to Rome with the popes of the Borgia family, knew how to use water in decoration. Thus the waters of Islam converged to the center of Christendom, along with the rediscovered gods of the ancient Romans, and they combined to produce some of the most splendid gardens in history. Perhaps such hybridity could only happen in a garden.[23]

The intention of these designers, of Donato Bramante, Jacopo Barozzi da Vignola, and Pirro Ligorio,[24] among others, appears to have been not so much to create gardens that were part of the house as to reduce the landscape to architectural proportions. One of the most endearing features of the garden at the Villa d'Este in Tivoli is its geometric, though nonacademic (in the current sense of the word) configuration, and its charming disregard for the natural contours of the hill on which it stands. At Villa Lante in Bagnaia, although natural woodland is combined with the garden, it is woodland tamed and graded, essentially artificial. But they remain for us today wonderful essays—Villa Lante in scent and texture, the Villa d'Este in sound and light, in dramatic contrast. One emerges from the peace of deep, or dappled, shade, to find great water gardens, alive with the light and music of dancing fountains.

If I am asked what the most important natural factor in the design of a garden is, I must say: it is light. Light is a thing that cannot be calculated, cannot be contrived. The use of light, when well thought-out, can bring surprising results. It is the constant change, the capriciousness, of light that makes the landscape architect's work so difficult and satisfying.[25] A painting cunningly hung can be made to appear handsome; a bad sculpture can be placed in the one position in which it looks good. But a careless form, an ill-considered volume, will be shown at once in a garden by a change in the light–the sun is very indiscreet. It can transfer in a moment the attention from some carefully planned point of focus to a shabby, ragged, disregarded group of shrubs.[26] Clouds, rain, and wind can change the appearance of a garden; its whole proportion can be altered when a sudden storm leaves puddles of water in unaccustomed places, or when the reflections disappear again from the wet surfaces.

A tree sunlit from above will look different in the evening, warmed and softened by the setting sun, which lights only the bark and the under surface of the leaves. Lit from the front, trees can seem solid, even sullen; with the sun behind them, they are light and translucent, elegant and witty.[27] A flower, a red peony or a rose, pale at midday, will glow and burn with an inner life in the long, soft light of a northern evening. Light never repeats itself.

In different parts of the world light has different qualities, it is the master touch of nature that suits her colors to her light.[28] In the Brazilian summer, when the light is blue and brilliant, we find flowering together *Acacia* and the *Tibouchina,* rich yellow and deep purples, suspended in a sea of saturated greens so intense they are almost black. In Japan, where the light is grayer, we have in spring the pure whites and the delicate pinks of the cherries, emerging from the misty atmosphere. In the autumn, with the clear scarlets and oranges of the Japanese maples (*Acer palmatum*) thrown into relief by the darkness of pines, which in certain light looks deep blue, all of nature seems to be burning. In the Alpine spring in Europe, when the light is liquid and pure, pale lilac, the flowers are white, pale yellow, mauve, and intense blue, cradled in the soft brilliance of new grass. **The important thing is to observe beauty in chromatic relationships.** "One can only look, and feel humble." Out of their context, those leaves, those flowers can be made to look vulgar, or anemic; within it, they have the perfection of simplicity. Man can do many things; but he cannot change or reproduce the light of nature. For who, in all its history, has been able even to describe, with pen or brush, the light of Greece? One must see to understand.[29]

But the garden makers of Renaissance Italy were occupied not only in bringing light and water into unexpected places, such as, for instance, the faces of unsuspecting guests. Certainly water was for them a wonderfully versatile material, which could be hurled into the air, which could tinkle or roar, gurgle and sigh, which could lie with the stillness of death or boil with unending white fury. In the garden of the Renaissance and of the 18th century, water was usually linked to sculpture, but in some of my gardens I have tried to give water itself the sensibility of sculpture, composing with the forms and rhythms of the jets. The movement and instability of water are symbolic of the very essence of garden composition: the cycle of life with birth, growth, and death, and the constant changing of the seasons. For water was rare in the landscape of central Italy; they had marshes but no lakes. They mainly tried to use water to impress. The fountain makers came to work more and more with sculptors; and gradually it was the sculpture that took over the Italian garden. From Isola Bella to Caserta, laid out as late as 1775, sculpture is the decoration that dominates.[30] It produced gardens that were always impressive; but to us they are not always gardens.

The word "baroque," in English, has often an uncomplimentary meeting. It has come to mean a style which disregards proportion; the whole extent of a garden was to be visible at one time. There could be no oddness of proportion, no divisions, no twisting paths, no sudden confrontations. Things of that sort could occur in the forest. Within the great design of the baroque garden, immense variety was possible, as it had been possible in the smaller gardens of the Middle Ages: but it was a variety completely subordinated to the demands of the whole.

Everything was combined to produce a sense of unity, a unity based on the use of the straight line, a unity that could be seen from any angle.[31]

The Portuguese word for baroque, *barroco* means an irregular pearl, that is, a pearl with an uneven texture. It is with this meaning in mind that we must approach baroque gardens, mainly those dating to the 17th century.

It is perhaps in Portugal that this type of garden can be best appreciated. There, lay Roman and Moorish traditions, subsequently perhaps marked with an Oriental influence. Again, the main patron would be the Church, which is powerful enough to destroy the old pagan names of the days of the week and replace them simply with words meaning "second day," "third day," etc.[32] But the results are completely different. The Portuguese produced gardens of modest richness, being especially skilled in contrasting surfaces–a wall of tiles, for example, emerging from a tank of still waters; whitewashed walls, highlighted by gray stone planks.

Their forms were rich, but their textures, visually at least, were simple. It was this style that gave Brazil many beautiful buildings and a wealthy tradition based on interconnected curves and contrasting, or complimentary, textures. There you will find whole church interiors carved and gilded over their entire surfaces; but because the surface is of a homogenous texture–the balance of these carvings is very delicate–the eye is never exhausted or distracted. There is no suggestion of overloading, and the shape of the walls and the arches is neither distorted nor concealed.

When clothing a garden, it is important to remember how disturbing unrelated textures can be. We live in a civilization that each day leaves us sorely in need of rest; the artist should no longer shock or stun. Thus, in the creation of harmony, the relation of textures becomes essential. In a natural forest, we do not find conflicting textures. The trees, adapted to the same physical conditions, all have leaves which, basically, either absorb or reflect the light. A natural forest is a pleasure for the eyes, especially when seen from above, because despite the different shapes and colors it contains, the texture of its leaves harmonizes.

To plant for flower color only is often very dangerous. We have all seen so-called blue "borders," made in the manner of Gertrude Jekyll, but without her taste and with many modern hybrids that she could never have used; whose leaves offer nothing but a constant battle; some shiny, some hairy, some spotty, some green, some gray, some long, some broad, some with purple veins, and others with yellow splashes, all presenting the effect that is patchy, incoherent–and anything but blue. A detailed knowledge of plant form and plant habit, which this kind of border is designed to display, is the beginning, and not the end, of a garden designers' equipment.[33]

In the gardens of Venus in Fronteira, we find the land covered with unglazed bricks, a wall of arcades and niches covered with glazed tiles.[34] The smaller niches contain figures, busts in bas-relief, contained in medallions; the roof is covered in dark unglazed tiles, similar to half a flowerpot. There is no undecorated surface, but harmony has been created because the textures seem skillfully correlated. In this garden, we can also see how a rectangular pool–which has some figures and a fountain, but hardly any other decoration–is located next to a topiary garden of the most elaborate kind.[35] The forms of the topiary are, however, discreet, rarely exceeding eye level, always related to each other and never isolated. It presents, therefore, a coherent surface, or texture, rather than a series of related forms. And this perfectly complements the plain surface of the water.

This type of contrast, on an enlarged scale, would give the great French gardens the sensation of space, which is their main characteristic. André Le Nôtre would adopt a master principle: the creation of perspectives leading the view to the horizon and suggesting the continuation of the garden in the distant landscape. The whole extent of the garden was to be visible at one time.[36] There would be no extravagance of proportions, no divisions, no winding or crossing pathways, no sudden confrontations. Within the immense layout of the garden, a huge variety was offered, as had occurred in the smaller gardens of the Middle Ages. But these were a variety completely subordinated to the demands of the whole. Everything should combine to produce a sense of unity, a unity based on the use of the straight line, a unity that could be seen from any angle.

The work of Le Nôtre must be regarded as the culmination of
the Renaissance style of gardening, brought directly from Italy. The
garden made by Francesco Primaticcio for Catherine de' Medici
at Montceaux-en-Brie, certainly offered the model for Vaux-le-Vicomte
and Versailles.[37] Here, enormous parterres, walled off from one
another, followed one another into the distance. In the wider, flatter
land of northern France, it was difficult to find a mountain to terminate
a vista; the vista had to become an object in itself. But it was an
outward-looking garden, the first in France; if not an integral part of
the landscape, at least it reached toward it. At Vaux-le-Vicomte,
a quadruple row of trees on either side simulated the forests that once
were there. These principles would be repeated later.[38] It appears
to have had an intimacy wholly lacking in the later gardens,
perhaps because it was made for a lady from Florence (de' Medici),
where gardens had been made in which to be pleasant with one's
friends.[39]

But Le Nôtre did not try to produce an intimate garden. His gardens
aimed to provide a sensational stage for a sensational play with the
audience both in the chateau and in the garden. His work is especially
remarkable for his handling of space, for his relation of one space
to another, and for his placing of volumes. There, whether a series
of fountains or a slightly raised parterre, whether a palace or a forest,
objects are always beautifully positioned. He brought to its highest
fulfillment the style of gardening which had been maturing through the
ages. With him, art reached a perfection of form and space. But it was
a fixed form subject only to variation; from it, no further development
was possible.

A revolution was required, and this was produced in England. Here
there was neither recent Italian influence, nor French; the formal garden
in the England of the 17th century was of Dutch provenance, as were
the gardens of Williamsburg.[40] Their principal legacy to the history of
gardening was to introduce a fondness for the growing of flowers,
a taste which seems to have been more common in northern Europe.
One will find flowers more often in the work of Lucas Cranach and
Albrecht Dürer than in that of Piero della Francesca and Leonardo da
Vinci.[41] The Dutch gardens from this time, which still exist in England,

at Hampton Court and Kensington Palace, are based on the use of volume and color. The gardens of which I have previously spoken were made with limited flowers; they were essays in space, volumes, and form, in harmony and contrast of surface and texture.

The landscape garden, in its original forms, was **made in reflection, and not in imitation, of the landscape.** The important thing is to understand the environment for which the garden is created. Imitation in art and especially in gardening is seldom successful. Even the most carefully imported foreign garden, slavishly imitated, rarely looks like anything but a slavish imitation, lacking the essential individual quality of a garden. The place for a Persian garden is in Persia; for a Japanese garden, Japan.[42] One can learn from the study of other gardens, as we can and should learn from the study of the inherent landscape–tonal sequence is very important in Japan, as is scent in Persia–just as one can and must learn from a study of the landscape. But while the landscape is there, there can be no necessity to reproduce it.[43] It should always be an aim to reflect the surrounding countryside, to plant in a garden the kind of plants that could grow in the landscape, plants suited both to the soil and to the climate. **A garden must belong, in spirit, to the ground on which it stands;** for, however carefully it may be designed, it will never look its best unless every plant within it is perfectly compatible.[44] It must always be an aim to make them so.

It was perhaps inevitable that the new kind of gardening should start in England. There, nature is essentially a domestic body, unlike the avenging, capricious goddess of the tropics, or even of the Mediterranean. Their landscape, too, had been cultivated for centuries.[45] If the garden were to complement the landscape, they had already made a landscape to complement their gardens. It is this tradition in which we principally work today. It has been much embroidered, overlaid, and overloaded, but in general the garden designer of today aims at a natural effect–an effect, that is to say, made by plants growing in a natural way, coaxed and cajoled, framed and groomed, but not regimented, not neglected, not forced into false shapes.[46]

It is in our capacity to use color that we chiefly differ from the early landscape gardeners; and **the successful use of color is**

one of the most difficult things in the world. One must go to great paintings of the present century, to the work of Georges Braque and Pablo Picasso; one must go the Impressionists, to Vincent Van Gogh and Paul Gauguin; one must look at the work of the Flemish tapestry makers, of the carpet makers of Teheran and Tabriz; one must examine the porcelain made under the great dynasties of China. Always one will find that the colors are related to each other in tone. Where one color is to dominate, it will be approached by gradations in tone; it will appear as the summit of a tonal sequence.[47] There is always a dominant color and dominated color.[48] **And a color will follow itself throughout a design; a color is never isolated, never alone.**

It can be difficult to resist the temptation of using too many colors; we have the opportunity of using plants from all over the world in every country. But it is important to remember that we are trying to produce a painting; we should never be content merely to assemble a fabulous paint box. It is important, too, to realize that all plants do not naturalize in all surroundings. In Brazil, we have the eucalyptus, the Australian *Casuarinas* (she-oak), the eastern plane, the rose, all out of place after a hundred years of cultivation; but the mango, the Barbados royal palm, and the flamboyant tropical almond (*Terminalia catappa*) appear perfectly at home.

Plants will always appear at their best when allied with plants of their own ecological grouping. I have seen in the Serra de Sincorá, in Bahia a most perfect natural garden. There, on graceful, wide, sloping shelves of golden rock, were growing *Clusias,* with shining dark green leaves, whose gloss and green were repeated by *Anthuriums* and by the leaves of certain orchids; there were golden, green, and grayish bromeliads, silver *Tillandsias* and one with a purplish stripe, tiny *Euphorbia,* small *Tibouchina,* some *Philodendrons* and some cactus. It was a marvelous symphony in muted tones, the colors a chromatic event, in which the volumes connected and established relationships, textures harmonizing with each other, all related to the smooth and glowing rock on which they grew.[49] There were intermediate planes between the slab and the valley background landscape; one could hear, at the bottom of the valley, the sound of falling water; but otherwise there was an enormous silence, peopled with the tiny, imperceptible sounds that make up the music of nature. The light around us was strong but never hard. Nothing was wrong. One might work for years and never achieve such a perfection of balance. This is the balance that was found in nature. A garden is organized nature, where the intention of the artist is to highlight the beauty of colors and forms, rhythm, and organized volumes. It means to establish harmonies, create contrasts, the whole being a web of elements, all indispensable.

Ideally, we should plant only species native to the area; but in some less-favored areas this might not produce a garden. Even for me, in Brazil, where I have a choice of five thousand trees and shrubs, there are limitations. With the richest national flora in the world, I have to borrow to find plants that will give flowers in flower beds.[50] I try to use flowers with a definite color that will not be drained by our strong, blue light. It is better not to grow a plant merely for the task of growing it; but if one decides to plant a plant that is obviously foreign, one should place it in an ecological group and then relate the whole group to the garden. One should remember that Capability Brown once planted 100 acres with only eight species of tree, to maximum effect; and that he worked principally with trees that were native to the British Isles, a very small group indeed.

It was work in this manner that first introduced me to the possibilities of the landscape garden.

About a hundred years ago, the French engineer, landscape architect, and botanist, Auguste François Marie Glaziou created in Rio de Janeiro the Campo de Santana and the Quinta da Boa Vista in the English landscape style.[51] He used paths and landscape elements in a way in which Brown might not have recognized; but his groups of trees in grass were in the true tradition of the English landscape garden, natural uprights in a natural surface, wide spaces and enormous simple volumes. One must admire the work of William Kent, particularly for his skill in the placing of objects–an urn, a statue, a temple; and of Humphry Repton, for the special subtlety of his textures; but it is from the work of Capability Brown that the landscape artists of today, as well as the designer of motorways, public parks, and crematoria, has the most to learn.[52]

One cannot create gardens by rules; to do so is to impose. In no branch of art should one impose; a work of art will always decide its own structure, a garden above all. A rule which can be made for one garden cannot be made for another. One can only try to arrive at certain principles; one must work by instinct, with imagination and intuition and, above all, with love; for to create a garden without love is to build a house of bricks without mortar. From history, one can accept the conventions of a garden, without ever being bound by them; from nature one can accept, in humility, her laws and her suggestions, acknowledging her always as the greatest artist of us all, with more to teach than can ever be learned. Let us, in an age of the scientist and the economist, never forget that.[53]

With a garden, one will always know if one is to compose a symphony or a simple motet. One must decide the key and the principle instrument; and, here one should be guided by the immediate surroundings, whether they are a sweep of unspoiled country or an ugly heap of urban constructions. The surroundings again will determine if the key is B major or minor; they will help to decide on the pace, the tempo—and whether an andante is to be followed by an adagio or an allegretto. Once this pattern has emerged, it is better to remain within it. One can change the key, but it must be to a related one; one can change from major to minor, but one must return again. To create a harmonic whole, each passage must be related. Where there are variations, they should be variations on a theme; and the rhythms should echo one another.[54]

One may think of a plant as a note. Played in one chord, it will sound in a particular way; in another chord, its value will be altered. Sometimes it is the keynote, sometimes a third related both up and down the scale; it can be legato, staccato, loud or soft, played on a tuba or on a violin. But it is the same note. A plant is a form, a color, a texture, a scent, a living being with needs and preferences, with a personality of its own. Distance and light change it, the wind will change it, rain and sun. Planted alone in grass it will have one value; in a group, among rocks, among differently textured leaves, in a colored plot, it will be different. We can think of a plant as a sculpture to be seen from many different angles;

to be transformed by a gust of wind, from tranquil green to a dancing figure of silver-backed leaves; to be spangled by the sun after a sudden shower. One may think of a plant as a brush stroke, as a single stitch of embroidery; but one must never forget that it is a living thing. One must try always to make it look as much like itself as possible.[55]

One can do this by contrast, in color if you like–colors, for instance, yellow and purple–but united by their leaf form, leaf texture, and by their height. Or three kinds of grass of different length and color, but of a similar texture. Or three different colors, each with its own texture, united in tone and size.[56] Or there are what I call analogies–leaves of similar shape but different color and texture, as of *Hemerocallis* (daylily) planted with *Neomarica* (walking iris), or *Kniphofia* (torch lily), or *Iris sibirica* (Siberian iris); or of a similar texture but different color and size, as *Heliconia* and *Ravenala* (traveler's palm)–here, too, there is an analogy of form. Then there is repetition, of a color, a silver agave planted beside a silver *Acacia;* of a form, different kinds of palm used in the same way. There must always be a link of color, texture, form, or scent. In the creation of nature, there is no such thing as an ugly plant: but by placing them wrongly, by ignoring their character, by contrasting them carelessly, or grouping them without consideration, plants can be made to appear ugly. And when this happens, it is only the fault of man.

The landscape architect in the 20th century is asked to do many things–to create a garden that will impress, or a garden which offers an escape, to make parkways, gardens of remembrance, botanical gardens, sometimes experimental gardens, which can be things of surpassing beauty. In the tea gardens of Assam, the tea bushes clipped flat to waist height follow the shape of the wide-spreading shade tree, *Albizia;*[57] in the coffee plantations of Colombia, the leaves of *Erythrina glauca* (coral bean tree) offer a beautiful contrast to those of the bushes below them.

But where the garden has a social function, it is important that aesthetics should also be taken into account: the first impression should be of a beautiful garden. I do not mean that the function should be disguised, or dissimulated. Disguises and dissimulations are soon discovered.

The function of the garden should be contained within its
beauty–it must not only be suited to its function. I have tried to do
this in the Flamengo Park in Rio; this park has two roads, playgrounds
and playing fields, a war memorial, restaurants, a museum of art,
a model aerodrome, parking lots, and a boating pool. So, it has many
functions. But above them the greatest seemed to me to be the recreation, within an urban context and around its social functions, of a
landscape that could have existed there–it is built entirely on reclaimed
ground. I have used plants that grow in the streets and on the hills of
Rio; I have related everything to something else, to produce a cohesive
whole. No form is isolated and I hope no form is ugly.[58] Already I think
it is an entity, a garden that also has social functions; and to create an
entity, I think one must always be consistent.[59]

Rhythm is not repetition; it is a question of relationship of one form
to another, one space to another, one texture, one surface, one color,
to another. Plants must be related to each other, including botanically
–a group of *Yucca,* or of *Philodendron,* or of Fabaceae.[60] It will be an
entity in constant change; but if it contains within itself the reasons
for being as it is, if all its parts are related, then it will always be in
harmony.

We fight, in some ways, a rearguard action. It is for the landscape architect to try and prevent the destruction of the
natural environment,[61] where it still exists; and at the same time
create new landscapes with echoes of the old landscapes, in order to
leave and establish an artistic legacy worthy of those who will come
after us.

One cannot always go to unspoiled nature for one's models.
Sometimes it will be impossible to avoid the creation of an artificial
landscape; but this, if it is consistent, need not be dishonest.[62] A
garden should be cohesive, complete in itself; and, if it cannot include
the landscape, it is better that it should reflect the landscape it comes
from. To meet nature undamaged is the privilege of the very few;[63] to
feel the expectancy of a forest as the sun begins to rise; to sense
the sigh of trees as darkness begins to fall; to hear the intense silence
of the mountains or the tundra, through which man merely passes.
There is the peace of God which passeth all understanding,[64] a peace

which man is gradually sweeping from the face of the earth. We shall
never re-create the peace of God; but we can try to approach it, to
create natural surroundings that can refresh and restore. It is not very
easy; there will always be people to destroy and to scribble all over
one's designs. But if, in the course of each day, even one person will
pause for a moment, and stand, and look, and feel renewed–then
that piece of work will not have been in vain.

To talk is easy, to do is more difficult.

Postscript

In my gardens, plants are usually the chief actors: plants with their
flowers and leaves, sometimes establishing harmonies and sometimes
contrasts of colors and shapes. As in other arts, the basic laws of
analogy and juxtaposition must be observed in composing with plants.
Certain plants will dominate only during certain moments. The
flowering cherry or our Brazilian ipê (*Handroanthus*) will dominate the
stage during an ephemeral moment each year; but at all periods
they will count as neutral backgrounds to other plants. As in architecture,
the relationship of space and volume must be carefully considered.
It is the interplay between small, medium, and large volumes, contrasted
or balanced, which will give validity to a composition. These are the
great lessons of Le Nôtre and Capability Brown. The compositions of
the past are for us to see, to analyze, to accept, or to reject. But I also
would like very much to say something that was not said before.

When we think in terms of gardens we cannot remain strangers to
new concepts of life and new formulations of principles of city planning.
In modern cities, gardens should be of central importance. Parks
with their recreation areas with safe walkways for children and the aged,
with areas in which the motor car can participate. Parking areas cannot
be ignored, but they have to be well solved, so that we don't have huge
areas of paving where the heat in summer is over-bearing and where
monotony leads us to hate the car, one of our most important means of
transportation today. The parks of our era must be intimately
connected with the technological problems of our times.

When I enter a modern city I cannot negate the possibilities of illumination resulting from a period in which electricity has modified all of our ways of life. In New York, or even in Rio de Janeiro, the neon signs, the advertising posters, the traffic lights, the lighting of parkways –these are not problems that can be ignored. From these is born a new aesthetics. The gardens of our grandfathers, the grottos, the pagodas, the ruins, all designed to evoke a past remembered with nostalgia, are not the matters of today. The garden has left the hand of the gardener, who although he may have had great knowledge of plant material was not solving the problems of the gardens of the modern city. All city planners view with consternation the growing megalopolis of our times, but we cannot be blind to reality. The function of the landscape architect today is to make known the part a garden has to play in the cities of our lives. He must struggle to retain what is valid, to put in evidence this great legacy which is nature. Resolving the problems of today, with knowledge, patience, and love, we will leave to those who come after us an inheritance which bears witness to the poetic meaning that we have been striving for our whole lives.

Text used for comparing the translation: Roberto Burle Marx, "O jardim como forma de arte," in *Arte e paisagem: conferências escolhidas,* ed. José Tabacow (São Paulo: Nobel, 2004), 51–68.

1   "…not merely one more way in which a successful egotist can add to his self-esteem. It is not a thing to be considered last when the money for a project has already been spent" is present in the English translation but absent from the Portuguese edition.

2   Mato Grosso is the third-largest state in Brazil whose dominant ecosystems include Cerrado, Pantanal, and rainforest.

3   *Paullinia cupana* (guarana), is a stimulant common in Brazil.

4   "goddesses" is present in the English translation but absent from the Portuguese edition.

5   Original (Spanish): *San Isidro, quita el agua y pon el sol.* "Saint Isidore, stop the rain and bring the sun."

6   Original: *conscientizados e puritanos.*

7   "God and…" is present in the English translation but absent from the Portuguese edition.

8   "and this has remained a constant feature…for their enemies to hide in" is present in the English translation but absent from the Portuguese edition.

9   A fresco of the Gardens of Amun in the Tomb of Sennufer, Thebes West, graveno. 96, depicts the four rectilinear ponds referred to in the lecture.

10   Original: *dedicado a um mito.*

11   "Decorative" was used in the English
     translation. This has been substituted with
     "aesthetic," which is closer to the
     Portuguese edition.

12   Pomona is commonly associated with
     the Greek goddess Demeter, goddess of
     the harvest and agriculture. Flora's Greek
     counterpart is Chloris, goddess
     of flowers.

13   "Grove" was used in the English
     translation. This has been substituted
     with "garden," which is closer to the
     Portuguese edition.

14   "Or merely suggested by a pergola; and
     lack of space also produced the roof
     garden, of which there is some evidence
     at Pompeii" is present in the English
     translation but absent from the
     Portuguese edition.

15   Pliny the Younger (61 A.D.–ca. 113 A.D.)
     mentioned the garden at Laurentum in
     a letter to Gallus, written around the end
     of the 1st century. Pliny the Younger,
     Letters, trans. William Melmoth, rev. F. C.
     T. Bosanquet (New York: P.F. Collier &
     Son, 1909–1914), vol. 4, pt. 4: letter xxiii.

16   Similar but not verbatim to a segment of
     a lecture also in this volume, *Gardens
     and Landscape.*

17   Original: *determinada finalidade,* meaning
     "a certain function / a single purpose."
     The English edition uses "social" instead.

18   "From them we can deduce that they…"
     is present in the Portuguese edition but
     absent from the English translation.

19   "The garden has always been…the
     swimming pool and tepidarium" is present
     in the English translation but absent
     from the Portuguese edition. A tepidarium
     refers to a Roman bath.

20   This is supposed to be a quote from
     Leon Battista Alberti (1404–1472), the
     Italian Renaissance architect and
     humanist, but Burle Marx does not
     mention the source.

21   Original: *compartilhava a formação
     do ambiente que o homem exigia para
     o seu lar.*

22   Presumably, this is also a quote from
     Alberti, but Burle Marx does not mention
     the source.

23   "At the same time, in the kingdom of
     Naples…Perhaps such hybridity could
     only happen in a garden" is present in
     the Portuguese edition but absent from
     the English translation.

24   Donato Bramante (1444–1514), Jacopo
     Barozzi da Vignola (also Giacomo Barozzi
     da Vignola) (1507–1573) and Pirro Ligorio
     (1513–1583) were Italian architects.

25   Original: "landscape gardener."

26   "…the sun is very indiscreet…
     disregarded group of shrubs" is present
     in the English translation but absent from
     the Portuguese edition.

27   Original:…*ela tornar-se-á escura,
     evidenciando a transparência de cores
     quentes.*

28   Original: *A luz se modifica; constitui
     o toque mestre da natureza, que
     estabelece relações cromáticas no
     decorrer do dia.*

29   "Man can do many things; but he cannot
     change or reproduce the light of nature.
     For who, in all its history, has been
     able even to describe, with pen or brush,
     the light of Greece? One must see
     to understand" is present in the English
     translation but absent from the
     Portuguese edition.

30   Both the Fountain of Venus and Adonis,
     Dolphins were constructed in 1775.

31   This paragraph is present in the English
     translation but absent from the
     Portuguese edition.

32   Portuguese days of the week are
     segunda feira (Monday), *terça feira*
     (Tuesday), etc.

33   This paragraph is present in the
     English translation but absent from the
     Portuguese edition.

34   Palacio de Fronteira, ca. 1671, Lisbon,
     Portugal.

35   Original: *se situa junto a um jardim de
     ávores podadas de maneira complicada.*

36   "The whole extent of the garden was to
     be visible at one time" is present in
     the English translation but absent from
     the Portuguese edition.

37   Burle Marx appears to be referring to the
     Palace of Fontainebleau in Seine-et-
     Marne, rather than Montceaux-en-Brie.

38   "These principles would be repeated
     later" is present in the Portuguese edition
     but absent from the English translation.

39   "It appears to have had an intimacy wholly
     lacking in the later gardens…in which to
     be pleasant with one's friends" is present
     in the English translation but absent
     from the Portuguese edition.

40   Original: *A attitude inglesa em face
     do problema jardinístico é bem diferente*

sobretudo no século XVIII, quando a paisagem existente e a contemplação da natureza iriam modificar basicamente a estrutura tradicional holandesa, como nos jardins de Williamsburg.

41 "One will find flowers more often in the work of Lucas Cranach and of Albrecht Dürer than in that of Piero della Francesca and Leonardo da Vinci" is present in the English translation but absent from the Portuguese edition.

42 "Imitation in art and especially in gardening is never successful.…The place for a Persian garden is in Persia; for a Japanese garden, Japan" is present in the English translation but absent from the Portuguese edition.

43 "tonal sequence is very important in Japan…there can be no necessity to reproduce it" is present in the English translation but absent from the Portuguese edition.

44 Original: *ecologicamente compatíveis.*

45 "It was perhaps inevitable…cultivated for centuries" is present in the English translation but absent from the Portuguese edition.

46 "It has been much embroidered…not forced into false shapes" is present in the English translation but absent from the Portuguese edition.

47 "Where one color is to dominate, it will be approached by gradations in tone; it will appear as the summit of a tonal sequence" is present in the English translation but absent from the Portuguese edition.

48 "There is always a dominant one and dominated one" is present in the Portuguese edition but absent from the English translation.

49 Original: *A textura das pedras se harmonizava com a das plantas.*

50 "With the richest national flora in the world, I have to borrow to find plants that will give flowers in flower beds" is present in the English translation but absent from the Portuguese edition.

51 Glaziou worked under Emperor Dom Pedro II as a landscape architect and engineer in Rio de Janeiro.

52 "One must admire the work of William Kent…has most to learn" is present in the English translation but absent from the Portuguese edition. William Kent

(1685–1748), Lancelot "Capability" Brown (1716–1783) and Humphry Repton (1752–1818) were pioneers of the English landscape garden.

53 "Acknowledging her always as the greatest artist of us all, with more to teach than can ever be learned. Let us, in an age of the scientist and the economist, never forget that" is present in the English translation but absent from the Portuguese edition.

54 "One must decide…echo one another" is present in the English translation but absent from the Portuguese edition.

55 "One must try always to make it look as much like itself as possible" is present in the English translation but absent from the Portuguese edition.

56 "Or three kinds of grass of different length and color, but of a similar texture. Or three different colors, each with its own texture, united in tone and size" is present in the English translation but absent from the Portuguese edition.

57 Spelling of the genus has changed within the past few decades; it used to be *Albizza* but is now *Albizia.*

58 "…and I hope no form is ugly" is present in the English translation but absent from the Portuguese edition.

59 "…and to create an entity, I think one must always be consistent" is present in the English translation but absent from the Portuguese edition.

60 Original: *As plantas devem ser relacionadas. É possível, inclusive, relacioná-las botanicamente num jardim.* The legume, pea, or bean family of plants, formerly known as *Leguminosae,* the term Burle Marx used.

61 Original: *região natural.*

62 "Sometimes it will be impossible to avoid the creation of an artificial landscape; but this, if it is consistent, need not be dishonest" is present in the English translation but absent from the Portuguese edition.

63 Similar but not verbatim to a segment of *Gardens and Landscape.*

64 "of God" is present in the English translation but absent from the Portuguese edition. Original: *Éden,* Garden of Eden.

Postscript is from *The Garden as an Art in Living,* in English translation.

The Garden as a Way of Life

The English lecture dates from 1967, and has some overlap
with *Gardens and Ecology*.

The purpose of the garden is to be a spatial condition
of community life: that is, to be a place which provides the desire
any man has to communicate with his fellow men, and with nature as
an aesthetic phenomenon and as a manifestation of life.

To organize nature according to a logic and a great decision of
the will is peculiar to the Southern spirit. To understand nature and to
integrate it with architectural creation in one organic composition is
peculiar to the northern spirit. In both cases, during the 17th and 18th
centuries, the garden was conceived as a composition of large spaces
and wide perspectives, and was also an art which encompassed all
others. Painters, sculptors, architects, poets, and philosophers were
dedicated to the understanding of nature and to the perfection of
its practice.

At the time of Louis XIV, the garden was mainly an expression
of royal power, a political instrument of prestige, and a display of
French hegemony, which through the talent of André le Nôtre reached
an independent artistic form and an insuperable creation of the era,
embracing the whole philosophy of the 17th century.

The vocabulary used at that time was relatively restricted, but with
the great botanical expeditions of the 17th and 18th centuries, it
has greatly expanded, chiefly with relation to ornamental plants. With
their wide dissemination, they acquired a great importance in the
garden. In the Victorian era, the garden became the responsibility of
the specialist in plants, the gardener, who knew the vocabulary quite
well, but who was not qualified to understand the garden as a special
problem. It was a time of floral arrangements, which looked like
magnificent wedding cakes and which pleased the ladies. There was
however, a new contribution in color, as for instance the mark of
Gertrude Jekyll, who used flowers in masses to create "flower borders,"
stands with high herbaceous plants in the background and smaller
plants in front.

The chief element in the composition of the garden is the plant, with
its whole biological complexity, with its different requirements, its form,
texture, volume, and individual coloring. But this does not mean that
the garden is a space full of plants: we should not forget its purposes.
There is the contemplative garden; the garden for meetings; the

one which considers the landscape and the one which excludes it;
the garden to be seen from above, as a chromatic composition;
and the garden to walk by. Furthermore, there is the private and the
public garden. But each problem has its specific characteristics, its
own planting conditions, and should be solved as such. In the following,
I will give some examples of gardens we have designed and the
policies which have guided us in each of them. In addition to the plastic
and landscape aspects, we have also considered the urban aspects
of these gardens.

Flamengo Park in Rio de Janeiro, a huge landfill area stolen from
the sea, bears precise urban purposes: to serve as a rapid outlet
for the traffic between the southern and central parts of the city, and
as a recreation area for the people of the neighborhood. We were
responsible for the project's gardens and we have planned, if not a
perfect integration of the park–divided by two high-speed lanes–a
sound distribution of the recreation areas, with model airplane strips,
model ship facilities, resting areas, and sport and parking areas.
In the park itself we proposed two different treatments: a more formal
garden connecting the architecture of the Museum of Modern Art
with the Monument to the Dead of World War II, and a free design
for the remaining area. Our intention was also to give importance to
the Brazilian flora by using the largest number of species resistant to the
sea air and adaptable to the climate. We considered, on the one
hand, that some plants are more expressive when gathered in compact
groupings, and on the other hand the parkway characteristics of
the Flamengo Park in order that these groupings have importance within
the landscape and may be seen when passing by in an automobile.
We have used trees with colorful blossoms in different seasons so
as there are variable centers of interest the year round.

Unfortunately I have to say that a misunderstanding on the part of
the persons who, due to circumstances, became responsible for the
development of the project, has caused poor results with relation to the
playgrounds, the lighting, and the great number of service stations.
This does not mean that we are unaware of the importance Atêrro do
Flamengo has to the city; we merely point out the facts to protest
against the adulteration of our work.

The Parque del Este in Caracas, an old coffee farm with beautiful trees such as *Erythrina glauca* (coral bean tree), faced us with another interesting problem: it should be a gathering and scattering place for the population of Caracas and a place for the preservation and maintenance of the Venezuelan flora. It included a Museum of Natural Sciences, a planetarium, sports area, an open-air theater, lakes with aquatic plants, places for the exhibition of fauna, as for instance aviaries and an ophidiarium,[1] as well as a restaurant and other attractions.

Important expeditions were made to the upper Orinoco River and to the basins of the Maracaibo and Canaima, with the purpose of collecting material for the park. There were several patios with special plastic-treated colors in the walls to match the plants, concentrated at the entrance: and using the preexisting species, a free design was given to the remaining area, by creating large spaces connected by paths in order to accentuate the surprise factor in the composition.

In the project for the garden of the quadricentennial of São Paulo (Ibirapuera Park), our intent was to make a showy, very exuberant garden, where, among other zones, we draw attention to the open-air exhibit of sculptures. It was planned in such a way that each work would be flattered by its surroundings. Green live walls or stone compartment walls of differing heights, varying according to the sculpture on display, isolated each artwork from the others and gave its due value in the space. In the locality of the lakes, water not only would serve as a vivifying element or as a reflecting surface, but also would be in itself a sculpture, falling in different-colored water jets, in different forms and heights and sequences. Although it has not been executed, this garden served as a new point of departure for our work.

There are also the national parks, areas which are considered of great landscape importance and places for the preservation of fauna. In these parks an intelligent management of the land is necessary. Groups of native trees strengthen the visual elements to create a valuable work.

But this criteria is not at all rigid, and depends on circumstances. In Minas Gerais, the Araxá Park was designed to be a spa due to the medicinal nature of its waters. We intended to treat the landscape

by using some knowledge of ecology, chiefly in the associations of
the plants among themselves and with the soil which supports them.
Here, we wish to pay homage to the great Brazilian botanist Henrique
Lahmeyer de Mello Barreto, a great and enthusiastic observer, who
took us to visit, one by one, the different associations of plants of the
Minas Gerais mountains. Together, we have analyzed the flora
of the sandstone, of the iron conglomerate, of the limestone, of the
granite gneiss; and we could observe that no plant has by itself
an absolute importance, because all the emotion it carries is modified
in relation to the other plants with which it is associated, and we
have verified that they acquire their importance as an expression of the
aggregate. We will discuss details of these aspects when we analyze
the problems of garden composition below.

Based on this experience and on others, we faced the questions
of the didactic gardens: the Botanical and Zoological Gardens of São
Paulo and Brasília, and the garden for the School of Architecture and
Urbanism of the Federal University of Rio de Janeiro.

In the Botanical and Zoological Park of Brasília,[2] the intention
was to create large flowery areas, with the necessary ecological niches,
by intensifying not only the relationship between the plants and the
soil, but also their association with the appropriate fauna. We proposed,
then, to create different zones of Brazilian flora: the Amazon, the
Atlantic forest, the xerophytes flora, the northeastern Caatinga,[3]
the thick woods of the Central Plateau, the Mato Grosso lowlands,
creating necessary ecological surroundings to allow placement
of various animals whose behavior would permit them to move freely
about the landscape. We also designed environments with European,
African, Asian, Australian, and North American flora, by using, obviously,
plants which could adapt themselves to Brasília's environment. For
the animals which cannot be allowed to roam freely, we have created
a special zoological garden where the habitats can be studied for each
one of them with the appropriate protection, either for the public or for
the animals, without the feeling of being in a cage.

The plants would be distributed, not according to strict ecological
or systematic criteria, but in line with a comprehensive idea which
would unite the harmony offered by the ecological with the need to

increase the value of the collection of certain groups systematically organized, to obtain a magnificent overall effect.

We also have another type of didactic garden which we consider of great importance to understand landscape architecture. It is the garden connected to the Architecture and Urbanism School of the Federal University of Rio de Janeiro to offer the students a rich landscape vocabulary, creating certain ecologic zones so that the student may notice the differences of the flora of the granite gneiss, of the limestone, of the iron and sandstone aggregate. There are lakes with a great variety of aquatic plants, surfaces which show the various soil coatings, and the differences in color and height, the garden of climbing plants, as well as the collection of palm trees, flowering trees, and bushes, distributed in an orderly architectural composition. We were able to show the shady plants, those which live in crevices, those which like the sand, the typical plants of the reefs; in brief, a wide variety, which will permit the students to get acquainted with the available vocabulary and use it as he wishes, getting away from established formulas of making a garden, against his own opinion, vocation, and principles.

Unfortunately, we cannot say that this garden, that we consider of great importance for the training of landscape architects, is a true school for gardeners, because it would be impossible to conduct botanic experiments on the garden; but our purposes have not been thoroughly understood. And, to add to this series of examples, to focus the points we tried to emphasize in each garden depending on its characteristics, we wish to point out the square.

We are now designing a square for the Curitiba Civic Center, a free space beside the State Government Palace, which compares only to Three Powers Square in Brasília among Brazilian cities.[4] Our intent is to unify the elements of this area, the various existing volumes, by other large volumes of trees: trees that are abundant in the landscape, as for example *Araucaria angustifolia* (Brazilian pine), which has a distinct structure and a characteristic shape. At the same time, we will use the traditional mosaic, which actually originates from the Romans, and bring the ground to life, creating contrasts of rhythm and color. It is a static surface, if we compare it with the surfaces of the three great lakes, with their aquatic plants, where water jets from different heights until they reach a climax: a liquid sculpture. Taking advantage of the possibilities made available by electricity, we will light the square through the great sprays of water to obtain all of the mutations of the reflection of light in them. And we will insist on the use of trees which bloom in several seasons, chiefly because in Brazil the seasons are not so well defined as here.

Once we consider the garden's implications as an artistic and urban phenomenon, we will analyze the aspects, not formulas, we consider effective for garden composition. We repeat, again, that we consider the plant the basic element of composition. In order to understand this, it would be necessary to understand a whole series of shapes which define it in space and in time. By analyzing it, we find a succession of necessary stages, dependent and supplementary: germination, growth, blossom, and fructification are phenomena that indicate a position in space and a projection in time.

Vegetation appears as a live, dynamic element, overcoming the apparent immobility of stone.

In the diversification of the Brazilian flora, we find plants that adapt themselves to all the possibilities of life, from the tree that grows almost without any earth on the stones of cliffs, to the extraordinary trees living in the swamps and whose fixing roots form the most unexpected arabesques and sculptures. The breeding roots, in turn, grow upwards and form a kind of a barrier. Examining the swamp in detail, it may be verified that the plant has characteristics of unbalance and adaptability, which makes certain plants, although taxonomically in different families, acquire a common denominator, an identity of expression. The plant also offers a sculptural aspect in its relationship with other materials, such as stone, water, sand—elements of a stable appearance which multiply their shapes. Or even the plant itself, by its definite structure, as for instance the palm trees, plants whose volumes, forms, and symmetry have importance in the landscape composition, and due to their columnar affinities serve through repetition for the modulation of rhythms, the delimitation of space, and the introduction of a significant verticalness.

The plant lives in accordance with the environment, and the conditions of the season to which it belongs connect to its requirements to be born, to grow, and to reproduce. In nature we find environmental solutions that will clearly express the life lived as a binomial form-function. We have not found associations as a simple accident: the compatibilities depend on a great number of factors, such as climate, soil, and the connection between plants, and among plants and animals. Ecologists call these groups associations.

The phenomenon of the association is closely connected to one of the most fascinating biological phenomena, which is adaptation. It would be impossible to discuss in depth such a vast theme; however, I feel that we can at least discuss here the mutual adaptation which attracts the attention of modern biologists and specialists on evolution, showing the simultaneous and associated improvement of flowers and of pollinating insects. In the beginning, in the Mesozoic era, the first plants with flowers were pollinated by rough, slow insects of the Coleoptera type (beetles). The evolution of the flower from this cyclic stage to the bilateral stage (orchids), or to the asymmetric (reeds), was followed by the appearance of quicker, more agile, and more specialized insects (butterflies and Hymenoptera–sawflies, bees, wasps, and ants). Also, the appearance of this high refinement: pollination by hummingbirds.

The extraordinary association of plants seem created to be united, one with the others. Studying with the great botanist Mello Barreto, I verified the "yoke" (iron conglomerate) flora in Minas Gerais: deep tones of yellow cadmium of the lichens and of the *Laelia flava* orchid, contrasting with the deep purple of the *Tibouchina holosericeae* (a low-flowering shrub) and in harmony with the Venetian red of the dorsal side of the leaves of the *Mimosa calodendron,* a plant known for the defense movements of its leaves.[5] Other times, we are impressed by the similar relationship and the supplementary nature of the features, as in the case of the granular *Tibouchina,* which is deep violet against the pink of the *Chorisiae,*[6] or the gold yellow of the *Vochysia* corresponding to the gold color of the *Jussiaea* (water primrose). This correspondence is extended to the relationship between the vegetable and the animal world. Thus, the bright red of the *Erythrina mulungu* (a tree native to the Cerrado and Caatinga regions) is projected in the color of birds like the *Tachyphonus* (tanager) and the *Ramphocelus bresilius dorsalis* (a tanager native to Brazil, with brilliant red feathers).

The convergence of forms is actually a simple expression of the laws of symmetry and growth to which the plants are subject, and which may associate beings that are far apart in the taxonomy, as for instance, in the inflorescence of the Costus (a large family of tropical flowers), whose overlapped bracts with their helical movement remind us of Coniferae (a division of conifer trees); or the case of the *Sipolisia*,[7] which looks like Velloziaceae (a family of flowering monocots); or the bromeliform *Eryngium* (sea holly) or the velloziform *Lychnophora* (a genus of South American daisies).

Discussing now the plant-rock adaptation, there is the impressive sight of the *Ceiba erianthus* (a prickly, deciduous tree that grows to 10 meters in height), which uses for its huge root only a small portion of the soil. It is the balance in the unbalance, as with the case of the *Ficus salicifolia* (a fig species of African origin) of the limestone, with their roots interwoven and their ability to evolve and dominate nearby supports, such as rocks, trees, and palm trees. Or the case of *Vriesea* (a genus of bromeliads), which is actually an aquatic plant living outside its environment but with its leaves arranged so as to serve as an aquatic deposit, or the *Tillandsia* (a different bromeliad genus, notable for its long leaves), which take humidity out of the atmosphere.

And now, we wish to point out the associations formed by plant and animal, as for instance, the pale-throated sloth (*Bradypus tridactylus*), which only eats the leaves of the *Cecropia* tree, or the mimicry that leads a type of butterfly to the gray trunk upon which she becomes undistinguishable.

This should be understood to be important for the preservation of our natural resources, but we feel discouraged to verify that the policy of razing the land is the prevailing one, everywhere, in a flagrant unconcern for nature: destroying in hours the work of a thousand years of evolution, modifying climatic conditions and microclimates, and causing the impoverishment of the soil and a destruction of the capital stock represented by the soil fertility. This entails the extermination of the fauna and the devastation of vast areas which are difficult to reclaim. It is an assault to the sources of life and a way to destroy future generations.

Conditions should be created in order to permit a presentation policy, through private, public, and international resources, of several reserves, with the main purpose of maintaining for the present and preserving for the future samples of nature in their primitive or less modified stage.

An idea we have been after for years is to start developing, with a staff of botanists and specialists, a garden where the plant, the animal, and the geology are part of a same ecological setting. We have proposed the Botanical and Zoological Park of Brasília: this way, the landscape architects would have available means of expression broader than the vocabulary they currently use in their compositions. The botanists developed their wide terminology as a result of the very vegetable forms, of the work of generations of studious observers, and it is this material that will help the landscape architect when he is to handle analogies and contrasts.

The rhythm of a leaf may have the significance of a painting, or a sculpture, in opposition to a stone or other volume. Sometimes to emphasize a huge leaf, we contrast it with a group of small leaves: those are valid and necessary options, because, if not, a formula would be created, and **formulas are always dangerous because they sterilize and create habits.**

The understanding of the aspects we have analyzed herein, and others which we may have omitted, will permit the garden-keeper to express himself in his own way, besides contributing to the maintenance of regional flowers.

We wish to emphasize that landscape architecture is an art;[8] however, a brightly elaborated art, which is the result of a web of concepts and knowledge, woven by the life of the artist himself, through his experiences, doubts, anguishes, tests, mistakes, and successes; but always with the intent of providing man with adequate places to enjoy life harmoniously, to communicate with his fellow men and with nature, **which we consider the real art of living.**

1   An ophidiarium is a snake house.
2   The Botanical and Zoological Park
     of Brasília remains unbuilt.
3   Caatinga is a type of stunted spare
     forest found in the drought areas
     of northeastern Brazil.
4   The Curitiba Civic Center dates from
     1966.
5   Similar excerpts appear in *Gardens
     and Ecology.*
6   The taxonomic genus name is now
     called *Ceiba.*
7   Now folded into the genus *Heterocoma,*
     the former *Sipolisia* is a part of the
     Aster family.
8   Originally, "landscaping."

Gardens and Ecology

The Portuguese version is dated June 1967; however, the unpublished English translation by Laurence Fleming is dated from March 1965. This lecture is primarily based on a revised translation by an unnamed editor dating from 1973. It was delivered at the University of Georgia, May 21, 1973 (hosted by the College of Environment & Design at the University of Georgia, and the Georgia Museum of Art); at the Massachusetts Institute of Technology, on May 23, 1973; and in New York, on May 25, 1973. The first publication of this essay was in 1969, Roberto Burle Marx, "Jardim e ecologia" (Gardens and Ecology), *Revista Brasileira de Cultura* (Ministério da Educação e Cultura) 1, no. 1 (July–September 1969): 29–35.

Supporters and opponents of all the theories of creation, no matter what their philosophical differences may be, agree completely on one point: that the appearance of life was not the consequence of a single act, but of successive stages. Genesis gives us details of these stages: the formation of the earth, the separation of the waters, the creation of plants, animals, and man. Science has now shown that plants, through a single chemical reaction, photosynthesis—in which they realized much earlier than Prometheus the dream of capturing the sun's rays—form the basis of the evolutionary process, changing the composition of the earth's atmosphere and allowing the existence of insects, birds, mammals, man, and even superior plants themselves, with all of their abundance of structure, form, and color. And it is plants that demonstrate to us most magnificently the phenomenon of the transmission of life, of reproduction, by the richness of their solution—the gala of flowering. One cannot repeat too often that the earth's atmosphere, with its 21-percent oxygen content, is a condition of life created and maintained by the activity of plants, principally algae.

The plant is our subject. And how does one consider a plant? On the one hand, it is a living being, obeying a conditional determinism through the laws of growth, physiology, and biochemistry. Any plant is the result of a long historical process, containing within itself all of the experience, joys, and sufferings of a long chain of ancestors, from its indefinable, primeval existence; and this perfecting of form, of color, and rhythm, and structure, makes the plant share with man another level of condition, a level of aesthetic being, giving to him a sense of mystery.[1] The plant has, in its highest degree, the property of being unstable. A plant is alive as long as it changes. It suffers a constant mutation, a lack of equilibrium which is in the end the search for equilibrium itself. The more we continue to examine plants, the more we continue to enlarge, almost in a logarithmic progression, the area of the unknown. Greater knowledge reveals greater mystery. The more we try to answer the question "how?" the more we pile up other, unanswerable ones: "why?" and "what for?" As an example, I may here recall a spectacle which I witnessed once in the Caatinga, in the northeast of Brazil. Here, at a certain hour of the night, over a large area, the *Cereus jamacaru* (cardeiro cactus) opened, in a hidden rhythm, as though guided by some unseen conductor,[2] their huge, white flowers. In brilliant moonlight, the many-petalled corollas opened slowly, offering their deep, white throats to thousands of insects. And watching them, I could not help but recall the movement of sea anemones and wonder at the unattainable reason behind this strange convergence. **Just as color is enriched by contrast with another color, so a plant assumes a new significance when placed beside another plant.** In nature we do not find associations merely as an accident. Compatibilities depend on a complex web of factors like climate, soil, and even interaction between plants and animals, or plants and other plants. The ecologists call such groupings associations.

The association phenomenon is closely connected with one of the most fascinating biological phenomena, that of adaptation. It would hardly be possible, now, to discuss such an immense and profound subject. However, I would like to speak briefly at least about the mutual adaptation so often mentioned by modern biologists and scholars of evolution, the simultaneous perfecting of flowers and of the insects that pollinate them.

In the beginning, in the Mesozoic era, the primeval plants and flowers were pollinated by rude, lazy, awkward insects of the type of the Coleoptera (beetles). The evolution of the flower from the cyclic stadium to the bilateral, as in the orchid, or to the asymmetric, as in the cane or reed, was followed by the appearance of more perfect, more agile, more specialized insects like butterflies and Hymenoptera (wasps, ants, bees, and sand flies), not to mention the highest refinement of all, pollination by hummingbirds.

On the surface of the earth no other region is richer in vegetal associations than the intertropical belt. This spectacle is much stronger and more impressive to the inhabitants of temperate countries in their first contact with the tropics. The amazing impact made by this world of tumultuous activity, of heat and life, colored forever the lives of many scientists from the period of the great discoveries: Carl Friedrich Philipp von Martius, Joseph Banks, Augustin Saint-Hilaire, Prince Maximilian of Wied-Neuwied, George Gardner, and many others. Even in our days, the richness of flowers in tropical zones is so impressive that I can report to you that I have never made a trip without finding or gathering plants completely unknown to me, some even unknown to science. As a result, it becomes clear that the garden is based on an ecological base, especially in a country like Brazil, with extremely varied conditions. For those who are concerned with the simple problem of introduction and cultivation, of domestication of wild plants, there is at their disposal a little-worked or even a virgin field in many of its aspects.[3]

Thus the landscape architect in Brazil is free to build gardens based on a floral reality of overflowing richness. Observing the demands of ecology and aesthetic compatibility, he is able to create artificial associations of the greatest expressiveness. To make artificial landscapes means neither to deny nor to imitate nature slavishly. It means, instead, to know how to transport and associate, with personal, selective judgment, the results of a long, loving, and intense observation. In my own experience, I can recall an apprenticeship served in close association with botanists, whose collaboration I consider essential to all people who want to devote themselves to the business of making conscious and profound landscape architecture, taking advantage of the immense heritage, so misunderstood by landscapers and garden lovers, that is the exuberant Brazilian flora.[4] In Brazil, although we have at our disposal approximately five thousand tree species—within a floral collection estimated at fifty thousand different species—our gardens exhibit above all a domesticated, cosmopolitan flora. Our streets are often planted with foreign species, such as plane trees or lavender bushes. I put away this concept of planting[5] and have fought with all my vigor against certain styles of town planning in which the natural landscape is completely destroyed in order to make, subsequently, a composition with plants that is completely divorced from the local landscape. What we destroy is the master work that represents a final condition, a stage of equilibrium in the million-year game of forces acting in nature. My conceptions arise, and my experiences proceed, from years of work understanding and interpreting natural associations; and one of those experiences was my observation of the Caatinga flora. Caatinga is a conglomerate of ferrous materials forming the soil of extensive areas in Central Brazil. Climbing the mountains, after traveling over extensive grasslands,

I came across a grayish spot of rocks and as I came closer a completely new world opened up to me. An extraordinary society seemed to have been created to form a complete reciprocal harmony.[6] The strong cadmium yellow of the lichen and the *Laelia flava* (an orchid) contrasted with the deep violet of the Quaresma trees, harmonizing with the Venetian red of the dorsal side of the leaves of the *Mimosa calodendron,* a plant that is also known for the defensive movements of its leaves. All of this polychrome is seated on a backdrop where form, rhythm, and color are in harmony, emphasizing at each season the character of a certain flowering. Nothing was isolated; it was an orchestra of color; the yellows linked to the blues, the blues to the violets, the violets to the pinks. One could speak, even, of a battle of color in which one color would dominate at a particular season, supported by a background whose forms, rhythms, and colors enhanced those of the plants in a very particular way.[7] This instability is precisely one of the great secrets of nature, which never tires us and is constantly renewed by the effect of light, rain, wind, and shadows, which shape new forms.

I also want to mention the limestone flora, whose rocks have a marked stratification and in whose cracks a rich biogenic sediment accumulates, where the roots will plunge, eager for the nutrients concentrated there. The spectacle is marked by groups or communities of palm trees (*Acrocomia aculeata*) and fig trees (*Ficus salicifolia*) with their interwoven roots and their special ability to wrap and dominate the various supports, such as rocks, trees, or palm trees. I have visited many regions of strange beauty. For instance, the Pancas Valley, which until thirty years ago still sheltered Indian tribes. This is a region of conical mountains, whose slopes are washed at the foot by the multitude of threading rivers and which shelter a flora uniquely their own—Velloziaceae, *Bombax,* orchids, *Mandevillas, Allamandas;* and to look at this valley, one would think it had been created by a theater designer. It is a pity that these primeval formations are not under protection, as a shrine is protected. They will be, in the end, destroyed by the local people,[8] who do not understand such treasures, or by European immigrants, transplanted but not yet adapted to the new world, who consider beautiful only that with which they were acquainted in their native countries.

And now I would like to tell you about one of the most striking vegetal formations of tropical America–the buritizal. The buriti (*Mauritia vinifera*) is the tallest palm of the Brazilian flora,[9] whose stem may reach 100 feet (30 meters) in height.[10] We can find communities of hundreds, or even thousands, in damp areas that are likely to be flooded. There are few examples of such a violent effort at perpetuation as that of their immense clusters, some yards long, composed of millions of berries, armored with copper-colored scales. Their leaves form a resting place for macaws which settle in them, like colorful flowers. The manner of propagation of this palm tree, whose fruits are carried by water, makes it grow in rows, sometimes rectilinear, following the course of the rivers. To make the buritizal image complete, more delicate plants grow among them, such as the buritirana–a palm tree like a miniature of the buriti– and the *Urospatha,* Araceae with arrow-like leaves and inflorescences of helical movement, which look like baroque ornaments.[11]

A plant lives in resonance to its surroundings and there is a connection between the conditions of the niche it inhabits and its requirements to be born, to grow up, and to reproduce. Vegetal life is a cyclical activity, whose pauses are marked by death and germination. This is a fact of crystal clearness for annual as well as for monocarpic plants like, for instance, the wonderful *Corypha umbraculifera* (the talipot palm), which takes forty to fifty years to produce a spectacular inflorescence, one of the most impressive shows in nature. It explodes into a pagoda of enormous cream-colored spikes, and the leaves take a second place in this fantastic display, which is entirely of their own creation.

Besides its general aspect, a region is subdivided into a succession of microclimates, deriving from various factors; topography, soil, altitude, etc., which from a gardener's point of view have the greatest importance. To make gardens, indeed, means sometimes to "create" microclimates, harmonizing them, remembering always that in these associations, plants place themselves side by side, as though the relationship were a necessity.

The value of a plant in a composition, like the value of a color in a painting, is always relative. A plant has more meaning when in contrast or harmony with other plants.

Speaking about the microclimate problem, I have been in a region where I could make valuable observations for my understanding. I refer to the Serra do Cipó, 100 kilometers from Belo Horizonte in the state of Minas Gerais, where the flora is chiefly defined by soils of quartz and sandstone. To undertake such a trip means walking from micro-climate to microclimate, from surprise to surprise. In each microclimate we meet plants that have changed so drastically under the action of forces common to that specific place that representatives of extremely separate families in the phylogenetic series have produced an accentuated similarity in their external appearance. Here, for instance, was *Sipolisia,*[12] from the composite family, with the shape of a *Vellozia* (a flowering monocot), *Eryngium bromeliaceae* (sea holly) and the *Lychrophora* (a South American daisy), also *Vellozia*-like. Here, as in other parts of Brazil (the Cabo Frio region, in particular, which is swept by strong winds blowing from a constant direction), we can observe the wind's modeling effect on plants. In sheltered depressions, trees grow in all their fullness and here, in this microclimate, an accumulation of humus remains and a greater retention of humidity keeps alive an unexpected world of orchids, lichens, and other epiphytes, which, although fond of humidity, do not want too much of it at their roots. In the most elevated points we find a peculiar community of plants, a nebulous flora characterized by small, apparently lopped trees with little leaves and an unexpected richness in epiphytes, mainly lichens, and harmonizing with them, orchids with deep colors, like the red flowers of the *Sophronitis.* Wisps of Spanish moss (*Tillandsia usneoides*) sway in the wind. It is a phantasmal landscape. Sometimes plants seem to dissolve and disappear in the mist; sometimes they appear in all their fullness when the sky clears and the light reveals successively different levels of flowerings.

Through these stops, on the same trip that I took with a dear and now deceased friend, botanist Henrique Lahmeyer de Mello Barreto, passed illustrious figures such as Auguste Saint-Hilare.

From the anthropocentric point of view, we may say that plants were created to serve man. This concept is expressed in the Bible. In Europe, with a highly domesticated flora, man kept a relative equilibrium with the trees and woods. But in conquering the New World, the forests, above all those of the tropics, filled his heart with terror. They were the refuge of all aggressive beings: the panther, the snake, the alligator, the spider, the mosquito, and the Amerindian with his poisonous arrow. He realized the necessity of opening strategic clearings, and the obsession for felling trees and destroying things began. The need for pastures and fields demanded enormous clearances. "Civilized" man assimilated the Amerindian *coivara*–the method of forest clearing through burning–previously used in concert with nomadic agriculture. Under European influence, *coivara* became more extensive and is now used with an intensity never known before, because the means of destruction–the machines, the bulldozers–become day after day more powerful. One of these monsters can destroy in a single hour the work of millions of years of evolution. This is the melancholy reality that enlightened people have to face. They are powerless to fight personally against the greater power of moral, economic, social, and psychological influences in the modern world.[13] Nevertheless, there remains a world of plant forms to preserve, a world that still remains little known owing to the shortage of methods and specialists. Our commercial way of life offers little reward for following the noble task of cultivating and preserving and disseminating the treasures represented by the plants of the tropical flora. The rapid and disorderly increase of populations presents problems of extreme gravity, including the shortage of arable soil. This does not help the public attitude toward conservation of nature and a respect for trees, and it seems that soon people will not know how to behave in a garden. But the dependence of man on plant life is so great that some feeling for it will remain.

In relation to the man-plant binomial, the dependence is so strong that, despite all incomprehension, it remains in feelings, in a desire for its presence. People, however, often like to exchange reality for appearance, as is shown by the present vogue for plastic plants and flowers. I saw the winter garden of an international hotel in Miami without a single living plant; everything was made of plastic. A big horticulturalist there had to close his model nursery because he could not compete with the manufacturers of pseudo-plants. There are millions of people who are not able to understand that a plant is something mutable, cyclical, and that its life means a succession of modifications which give the enchantment you can never find in an inexpressive, static plastic model.

I should like to insist once more on the theme of devastation, which is more serious in tropical countries than in temperate ones. I wish to point out that its principal effects are climatic and microclimatic changes and the destruction of a common capital represented by the fertility of the soil. The suppression of the flora and fauna and the transformation of areas into deserts is hardly a reversible process. It represents a human attack against the sources of life and a form of destruction of future generations.

The social mission of the landscape architect has a pedagogical side of communicating to the masses a feeling of esteem and comprehension of the values of nature through his presentation of it in parks and gardens. In Brazil—where there is sometimes a suspicious aversion to local plants, a preference for foreign ones over what are considered to be weeds—I have had, over long experience, to insist again and again, against much opposition, on a fuller understanding of the importance of our action and our contribution to changing the public's mentality. We should show that someone was worried about leaving a valid aesthetic and useful legacy to those who come after us.

Prevailing conditions in Brazil, and possibly in other tropical countries, allow us to delineate a preservation policy of what still exists, by creating, with private, public, and international resources, a series of reserves with the main purpose of maintaining samples of nature in its primitive or even slightly altered state, both for the present and for the future.

Considering the diversity of the flora, these reserves, real natural botanical gardens, should be distributed over different botanical provinces, preserving as many precious local communities of plants as possible. The landscape architect would thus have at his disposal broader means of expression represented by what is, to them, a vocabulary with which they write their compositions. With this abundant reservoir of expressive material one should guarantee possibilities to create the great works of which the creative mind of man was and is capable, using the laws of aesthetic composition, the laws of contrast, harmony, and proportion. Idea gives form to substance but it is necessary that there be proper substance to embody the idea.

In concluding this lecture, I wish to state firmly that the creation of gardens is an art, an art which uses as its chief material the living flora. In the contemplation of nature, with its endless variety of forms, the artist finds stimulus and inspiration. Based on his observations of the needs and functions of certain plants, he regroups them to fulfill an aesthetic need. So the garden is highly elaborated, resulting from an arrangement of conception and knowledge of natural materials according to aesthetic laws; and interwoven with this are the artist's outlook on life, his past experience, uncertainties, afflictions, attempts, mistakes, and successes.

Original text used for comparing the translation: Roberto Burle Marx, "Jardim e Ecologia," in *Arte e paisagem: conferências escolhidas,* ed. José Tabacow (São Paulo: Nobel, 1987), 37–44.

1 Original:…*cuja existência é um mistério para o homem.*

2 "…as though guided by some unseen conductor" is present in the English translation but absent from the Portuguese edition.

3 "As a result…a virgin field in many of its aspects" is present in the Portuguese edition but absent from the English translation.

4 "…taking advantage of the immense heritage, so misunderstood by landscapers and garden lovers, that is the exuberant Brazilian flora" is present in the Portuguese edition but absent from the English translation.

5 Originally, "landscaping."

6 Original:…*essa extraordinária associaçao de plantas…*

7 "Nothing was isolated; it was an orchestra of color;…enhanced those of the plants in a very particular way"

is present in the English translation but absent from the Portuguese edition.

8 Original: *gente da terra.*

9 Original: *palmeiras,* translated as "palm tree" in English. However, palms are, strictly speaking, not trees on account of not having cambium, having an adventitious root system, and rarely having branches, with the leaves emerging directly from the stem. See Roy Ellen, "Palms and the Prototypicality of Trees," in *The Social Life of Trees: Anthropological Perspectives on Tree Symbolism,* ed. Laura Rival (Oxford, U.K.: Berg, 1998), 59–60.

10 Original: *50 metros = 164 feet.* The correct number should be between 20–35 meters (Embrapa), or 100 feet.

11 This paragraph is present in the Portuguese edition but is absent from the 1973 English translation on which this text is primarily based.

12 The taxonomic genera of *Sipolisia* was folded recently into *Heterocoma.* They are members of the Aster family.

13 Originally "violence," rather than "power."

architect
~~gardener~~ It may seem strange to you, that a landscape
from the Tropics should come to propose to you,
who live in a conntry with Northern tradition and a Northern
climate, solutions which, in the past 20 years, he has
been seeking for gardens in Brazil.

Yet these experiments have interested landscape
artists and architects who do not work in the tropics,
just as it seems that Brazilian contemporary architecture
at times successfully, but sometimes less so
has suggested solutions adopted by architects in quite
different climates and under differing social conditions.
The garden I designed for Mrs. Tremayne, with flora suitable
to Santa Barbara in California, was never laid out, but the
colored chart for this garden was exhibited both in your
University and is a permanent exhibit in the Museum of
Modern Art of New York, and has brought me many letters
that suggested that people all over the world are seeking
solutions to a problem identical with my own - that of
finding a garden style to meet contemporary needs -

artistic, social and economic, for the man in the city as well as the country-dweller. 10 years ago, in "Brazil Builds", Philip Goodwin published some of these solutions, made in collaboration with our new generation of architects, inspired by Le Corbusier's visit to Brazil: and an article which appeared in the London "Architectural Review" in 1947 suggested that "once the idea of the contemporary garden, planned according to Burle Marx's principles, has been postulated, its variations need have no limits".

What these simple basic principles are, and how I have carried them out in a tropical climate, is what I hope to illustrate during the course of this talk.

But first of all, what does a landscape architect like myself understand by a garden ? There are many public squares with beaten earth and a few unpainted benches and one or two old trees which have not as yet been uprooted, which are still called gardens, but are not worthy of the name.

A garden in its wider sense is, I think, a careful selection of certain aspects of nature, water, rock, flower, foliage, ordered and arranged by Man, and in which Man may have direct contact with plants; an area in space, however small, in which he may find rest, relaxation, recreation, and above all the feeling that he is living in, and integrated into, this space. It is also a complex of plastic intentions, with a utilitarian purpose: and it should, whenever possible, fuse with the surrounding landscape, whilst being an extension of the architecture for which it is designed. For instance, it may be a roof garden where workers in the office building

hoto of
of Min.
ation

can spend their lunch hour, a collective garden for an appartment building - and in this case it shouId be plante d with hardy sculptural plants, in order to stand exposure to strong winds, and in order to complete the architecture with smaller but decorative contrasting volumes. If, in the case of a public square, it is not designed to be the continuation of the architecture, then it should have architectural characteristics of its own - say, an acoustic shell for music, attractively designed benches for those who sit there, a mosaic-faced pool, or a pool backed by a wall with a mural - something to arrest the interest, and create pleasure and surprise. But above all, it is a place in which the plant is the dominant element, chosen and placed not mechanically and according to a standard specification, but in such a way as to produce constant exaltation in the visitor. I stress this point because so much importance has been given lately (and understandably) to constructional materials (wood, concrete flower boxes, and so on) which simplify the general upkeep and reduce staff-costs of gardeners both in private and public gardens, that the plant, the <u>chief actor</u> in the spectacle, is gradually being imprisoned on smaller and smaller stages, and the feeling of growth, of pulsating life, is being stifled. This does not mean, that the free-standing wall faced with mosaic of blue glaze tiles, which I use for privacy or windbreaks as well as with aesthetic intention, or the granite or stone slabs used for paths, benches, sculptural elements, do not have their legitimate place in the contemporary garden - but anyone who has stood in the shade of a constructed wall, looking out onto the garden, and then has moved to the cooler shadow of an overhanging

Photo of
.iage
utherot)

Photo of
lther Mo-Aizm
ira Salles
ulejo Wall

tree, knows the immense physical and aesthetic difference -
there is life in the shade of a living tree - life in the
colors and shapes one perceives, under its protection.

Then, too, a garden is Man's conception of Nature
as she presents herself to us. (In England, where much of
the so-called natural scenery is a legacy of the brilliant
landscape gardening of the 18th century, this statement may
not seem entirely accurate, but in Brazil, where even today
in unexplored regions Man is fighting a hostile Nature,
cutting and burning before he replants, the jungle has little
similarity with a garden. It is true that Nature has her own
sharply defined laws, which tell of a close interrelation
between trees, plants, animals birds and insects. In the
Amazon Basin there are parrot-hued heliconias with bracts
which might well be parrots' beaks, both as regards their
color and structure; there are grasshoppers which might be
leaves in the wind, butterflies which might be orchids and
orchids which might be butterflies; and during a hunt which
I once unwillingly witnessed, organized to shoot down little
green parrakeets, when these fell to the ground the soil
seemed strewn, not with dead green birds, but with living
green leaves. And though there exists an interdependence
in Nature, there is also a constant fight going on, one
plant or animal striving to survive, to assert itself, at
the cost of weaker elements. Whereas in a garden, it is the
landscaper who decides which shall be the dominant plant,
at least in the period of creation and execution.

Of course, he may decide, for some definite demonstrational and didactic purpose, to reproduce in miniature,
some plant or animal life complex, depicting as faithfully as

possible, Nature in her original state. That is just what
I did, in collaboration with the great botanist Henrique
Lahmeyer de Mello Barreto, now head of the Federal District's
Zoological Garden. We reproduced one section of a park designed to be a prototype of the vegetation and bird and
animal habitats of the Federal District - that which is the
home of marsh birds. And we had the wonderful experience of
finding that, in this habitat, not only did the plants and
the birds both thrive wonderfully, but that other wild marsh
birds, whose homes are vanishing as the marshland is being
reclaimed, had flown in from far off, and joined the colony !
Such an experiment is, however, both impossibly expensive
(not even in the Zoological Gardens could we carry out the
entire project) and, in addition, the island was planned for
the birds, for scientific experiment, more than for human
beings.

The planning of a garden must take into account
the purpose for which it is being designed, as also the
locale. (Obviously in the marsh bird complex I mentioned, no
cactus plants would be planted, nor would one put a rosebush
at the edge of a pool devoted to the Victoria Regia) The size,
the shape, the chief characteristics, the proportion of plants
in relation to constructional elements, will depend on the sort
of people who are going to use the garden. A children's garden
such as the one at Pedregulho Housing Scheme, will need sand,
and areas where recreational appliances may be placed, and the
plants must be hardy to stand up to rough usage; a garden for
old people will need benches strategically placed, in sun and
shade, with elements of higher aesthetic interest: water pools,
mosaic paths, tiled wall murals, fountains or statuary. And

Extract from typed manuscript of *Finding a Garden Style to Meet Contemporary Needs* with handwritten annotations by Roberto Burle Marx. The lecture was delivered at the Harvard University Graduate School of Design in 1986.

Gardens
and Landscape

Undated lecture.

Since the very beginning of history, gardens were intimately related to man. When man stops being a nomad, he tries to limit space by means of hedges and walls. Within that limited area, he plants what is necessary to his subsistence and starts to develop a selective knowledge of certain elements of the flora. He selects plants that are medicinal, others that have a magical or religious significance, and even some that appeal to him because of their shape or color.

Since then the flora has always been present in human and social activities. As an example, it is enough to consider phytomorphology in architecture:[1] the lotus-shaped capital of the Egyptians, the acanthus leaf of the Corinthians, and an infinite number of other examples in the course of history.

People express themselves through elements coming from their environments and, according to their needs, build gardens and parks, the purposes of which are diverse. The squares of medieval cities were sites for commerce, for theatrical presentations, or simply social meeting points. The gardens of the Château de Versailles, built in the 17th century, played a political part in the process of the unification of France: by means of the festivities presented there, Louis XIV forced princes and potentates to remain at court for long periods, while political maneuvers took place.

The park of Versailles gives evidence of André Le Nôtre's Cartesian mind. In the clearings, enhanced by lakes and canals, one can see clearly the hedges that limit the woods. Contrasting with the dark green foliage marble sculptures—sometimes of doubtful quality—are set rhythmically.

On the other hand, the British tried to bring landscape within their parks. They avoided hedges or walls that would limit space. Hampton Court and Blenheim show an inventive spirit, the creative minds of Humphry Repton and Capability Brown reaching the highest level.[2] Using a few species of trees forming large groups of the same plants, they managed to characterize blooming, massive shapes, and fit too wide items to scaled ground.

The 19th century is remarkable for the increase in the search for plants. Commercial nurseries of Britain, Germany, and Belgium, amongst others, sent botanists and plant collectors to Asia, Africa, and America, with the purpose of increasing the gardener's repertoire.

Commercial competition was such that, for the purpose of keeping their collections exclusive, certain cultivators gave wrong information about the provenance of plants. This has caused, and still causes, great problems in the field of systematic botany.

In that period, Brazil was revealed to the world through *Flora Brasiliensis,* by Carl Friedrich Philipp Von Martius, et al., the immortal monument to which about sixty-five botanists and a great number of draftsmen gave their collaboration over the course of almost a hundred years. They crossed the country in diverse directions, enriching our knowledge amazingly, discovering a great many plants that figure nowadays in gardens the world over.[3]

When Art Nouveau appeared as a reaction against an academic attitude, the artist turned again to nature for inspiration. The stylized transposition of flowers, leaves, and butterflies became dominant. The new possibilities created by the Industrial Revolution brought profound changes into architectural concepts.

Yet it seems that man was not prepared to apply consciously and nationally the technical developments that followed the Industrial Revolution.

Cities have grown vertically but maintained a road structure meant to serve one-family houses. The rural exodus favored speculation in urban land, since the demand for city dwellings rose out of all proportions. Quality of life declined swiftly, and chaos set in. Nowadays man builds cars that can go 120 miles per hour, and in them he takes half an hour to cover 1 mile, while inhaling smoke and putting up with insults.

Nature has been gradually forgotten. The green areas left in town were, little by little, used for building schools, hospitals, libraries, or simply retained and sold, as proof of thoughtlessness and greed. With the super-valuation on city land, families that needed to have their gardens and orchards were reduced to cultivating plants in pots on the kitchen window. Man proved so far away from nature that his idea of her deformed, and he became satisfied with plastic plants.

The situation having reached a critical point, there had to be a reaction. Planners in urban matters started worrying about the need to maintain free spaces within an urban context. New laws were proposed in order to rationalize the use and occupation of the land. Squares and parks of communal use made their appearance. And there was a battle between conscientious legislators and real estate speculators, all of them firmly disposed not to give way an inch.

In Brazilian towns, that battle still goes on. The real estate industry tries to justify itself by the great number of jobs it originates, ignoring the quality of living and technical requirements. The buildings are like huge cakes whose outward appearance is perfect, but the inside is rotten. The buyer only finds that out when he tastes the cake. As I said before, the demographic density is too high for the urban infrastructure, overloaded and obsolete.

Fortunately, I notice that, nowadays, there is an affinity between city planners, landscape architects, and architects, so that they all want to guarantee the open spaces to which man is entitled.

Nowadays, such areas have a priority in any city-planning project, in which there are always included spaces for playgrounds, playfields, picnics, sports, meditation—in short, for active and passive leisure. There are also areas for cultural improvement, such as open-air theaters, botanical and zoological gardens.

This trend expresses the desire of man to return to living close to nature. But even that becomes more and more problematic. The devastation that the land has, and still is, suffering, frightfully reduces our possibilities to live in the natural environment. We are the only animals to destroy the natural environment in which we live and on which we depend. And certain interferences have already caused alterations so deep as to be irreversible. My knowledge in that field is limited to the Brazilian soil, which I have learned to love and to defend.

I have made countless journeys through Brazilian hinterlands, searching out new expressions. My purpose is to discover new plants in order to broaden the means of expression of the landscapes. Besides that, in such trips I observe the plant in the habitat of its associations, conditions of light and winds.

Together with the botanist Henrique Lahmeyer de Mello Barreto—with whom I learned so much about observing nature—I managed to select plants never before used in gardens, but which have their utilization fully justified because of their shape, blooming, volume, or structure. Once they were used, those species have acquired commercial value, and plants formerly despised started being avidly hunted. In fact, it is interesting to observe that many Brazilian plants began to be used in Brazil in a spirit of imitation, as soon as they were noticed present in European hothouses.

The conclusions I deduced from the many journeys I have made through Brazil have been most valuable to me. A few months ago I went to the Plateau of the Veadeiros, 200 miles north of Brasília. There I traveled through country of extreme beauty. Rocky banks of sandstone and silica exhibited large formations of *Vellozia glauca,* associated with an *Allamanda* with narrow leaves and an *Euphorbiacee* with bluish leaves and pink veins. Complementing by contrast the scheme of colors, there was the golden yellow of the dry grasses that covered the soil. In that region, in the low or depressed spot where water accumulates, grow groups of buriti, huge palm trees with large fan-shaped leaves, which live in association with the buritirana, of much smaller size but with the same shape. The seeds, carried by the watercourses, germinate further down and in that process come into being the lines of buritis that clearly mark the run of the brooks.

When I design gardens I don't try to copy nature slavishly. But there are several examples–like that of the buriti–which may and must be used as elements of composition. That is what I have been trying to do, and I may consider the results as positive. Through observation I was able to conclude that, by employing those lines, we can direct the spectator's sight to a determined point we wish to emphasize.

By observing the formation known in Brazil as Cerrado, I obtained several elements that I started using in my compositions. The Cerrado is home to the most spectacular transformations that nature can provide. After a six months' drought, when most of the plants are leafless and the only colors are the ochre of the soil, the thorn and limbs of the trees, with the full fall the Cerrado comes through.

In the rainy forests of the seacoast of Serra do Mar, humidity is permanent and consequently, so is foliage. Observed from a distance they appear to be of an even green, almost black. But when one enters those forests, one is surprised by the intricacy of the vegetation. The richness of the undergrowth and of the epiphytes is immeasurable. The constant damp, and the protection coming from treetops that filter the sunlight, make the environment favorable to the development of the epiphytic flora, represented there mainly by plants from the families of Orchidaceae, Araceae, Bromeliaceae, Cactaceae, Piperaceae. Dominant in the undergrowth are the Musaceae, Marantaceae, and Begoniaceae.

The sight of that association of plants gives us the impression of a covenant for living together. Here, even competition is balanced. Each being struggles for the minimal conditions necessary to its survival. No epiphyte wishes to possess alone a whole tree. Quite different from man. The general feeling is that of balance.

It is that balance that I have taken into consideration—at the same time as trying to emphasize the characteristics of certain species—when I started to use large groups of the same plant in parks. This way, the observer can better distinguish the peculiarities of each, because he is free from the competition and visual confusion that come when different species are mixed.

I am aware that in nature one can find a different plant dispersed amongst others, but when I compose a park or a square, I am bringing order, so as to make nature more accessible. And speaking from experience, I can say that the plant used in large groups becomes easier to comprehend.

Here I must mention that most impressive formation: the Amazon forest. Covering about 45 percent of Brazilian territory, stretching to Peru, Bolivia, Ecuador, Colombia, and Venezuela, that forest has always been menaced by attempts at occupation. There, Henry Ford invested millions of dollars in rubber-tree plantations, and did not manage to get even 1 gram of rubber. Other businessmen tried systematic plantation of Brazil nuts, but they were never fruitful.

I believe these examples illustrate the complexity of an ecological system that has been very little studied. The same sort of tree can subsist in dry land or in flooded areas, where it becomes adapted to having the trunk submersed, sometimes to the extent of 13 yards. The relative humidity of the air is continuous, which accounts for

the frequency of large leaves. The vegetation is always exuberant
and heterogeneous, presenting wide variations between two different
areas.

However, to the contrary of what most people suppose, the soil is
not fertile. The organic coat is quite shallow, and the soil below is sand.
Reaching for the sunlight, the trees grow very tall, and lean on each
other, since the root systems are usually superficial. Once a tree is cut,
it is common to have two or three which leaned upon it fall down. The
whole system hangs on a delicate ecological balance.

Another phenomenon common in the Amazon is that of floating
islands. Large chunks of soil get loose from the river's edge, and float
down to the sea, disintegrating little by little. They carry big trees,
palms, monkeys, snakes, etc. Here, once again, we find man adopting
solutions from nature: it is common to see boats towing rows of rafts
with houses built on them, chicken coops, and even small gardens of
potted plants–generally plants from other regions, with foliage brightly
colored, almost a psychological reaction against the intense domination
of green in the environment.

In only one lecture it would be impossible to give a detailed
description of the scenic aspects of the Brazilian landscape. However,
the examples given serve to illustrate one of the most important
principles that guides me when I design a garden: the understanding of
the characteristics of a natural formation. I consider that indispensable
to those who intend to design gardens.

Gardens are works of art, and have to be treated
as such. As in painting, sculpture, and architecture, we have to bear
in mind color, texture, volume, and form. Yet there is a requisite
to gardens that we do not find in other works of art. That is instability.
Even if a garden is built, it is not finished. Plants have to live before
they reach the required volume. Besides, there is the mutation, periodic
and cyclic, in the course of the year: that is, flowering, fruit bearing,
and fall of leaves. Finally, there are changes in the course of the day:
light, atmospheric conditions, and other aspects. All that, while
almost imponderable, must be taken into account in the designing of
a garden, which I believe must start from an impulse controlled and
limited by principles, not by formulas or recipes.

Those who intend to build gardens have to keep in mind the principles that guide a composition, and use self-control to avoid the mistake–so common amongst beginners–of trying to apply the whole of their knowledge to one single garden, sometimes of a small size. It is important to select and dramatize certain passages of a composition by means of plants creating elements of surprise; regulating small, medium, and large volumes; or using more insistently one certain plant, so as to bring out its characteristics to give them value. What is essential is to have in mind a composition in which there always must be one dominant and one dominated, without forgetting the elements of color, form, rhythm, and, above all, the relationship of volumes.

By and large I have talked about the concerns I have when I design, but I **must still emphasize the importance of the program in a landscape project.** It is obvious that a garden for a motel will be different from a garden for a convent. The landscape architect must concern himself with studying the requirements of the projected garden so as to select elements to make it worthwhile.

What I tried to explain in the statements above is the way I look at landscape problems. A project may be rich in functional solutions, but it will be incomplete if adequate vegetation is not provided.

It was because of that concern that I devoted myself to collecting botanical material; for, through the growth of the botanical repertoire, new possibilities of expression turn up. Academic conventionalism has always existed. Yet if we observe the plant in isolation or in association, we may discover in it a totally new significance: thus the importance of getting from the existing landscape the elements necessary to the built landscape. Japanese gardens illustrate well what I mean. They are transpositions, sometimes reductions, of an existing landscape, where the artist has searched for his means of expression. In those gardens one notices the intention of considering the milieu as a whole, for it is impossible to set definite limits. Continuity has to be maintained. For example, I might say that it is impossible to draw a line where the urban landscape ends and where the rural begins. It is obvious that there is a transition zone, but that does not break continuity.

In Brazil, due to the variety of landscape aspects, I felt I had to know and utilize the flora in that same spirit.

And I had to fight for its defense and survival. In my country home I have experimented with adapting plants brought from the most diverse environments. There I have representatives from the coastal flora, from the mountain slopes, the Cerrados rocky hills, and the Amazon forest; and, dealing with them, discovering their needs and affinities, I learn a little more about the way they live, and their life cycle.

It was the exercising of those activities that made me understand that the mission of preserving the landscape—at least as I see it—goes beyond the work of composition. **One must bring nature into the reach of man and, above all, take man back to nature.**

1   Phytomorphology is the study of plant form.
2   Capability Brown (1716–1783) and Humphry Repton (1752–1818) were pioneers of the English landscape garden.
3   The 10,367-page *Flora Brasiliensis* contains descriptions of almost 23,000 species, in 15 volumes, with 40 parts. *Flora Brasiliensis* was edited by Carl Friedrich Philipp von Martius, August Wilhelm Eichler, and Ignatz Urban, and about 65 other botanists from various countries. The research was conducted between 1840 and 1906.

The Plant

Undated lecture.

Although what I am going to say is drawn from my own personal history, in fact the Plant is the main character.

Plants have always been an integral part of my life, through the influence of the two mothers I had the good fortune to have–the real one and another, who helped to bring me up. I remember very clearly my mother pruning roses on sunny mornings in the winter in São Paulo, and my own interest in those skeleton plants, which after some days would give buds and later flowers.

Another strong impression that I still have is of the begonias and caladiums which, imported from Pernambuco where my mother grew up, were grown in hothouses with real love, the principal and indispensable quality for anyone who wants to grow plants.

Later, my other mother, Ana, introduced me to the art of planting seeds and the pleasures of cultivation; and I can still remember the delight of taking out of the ground the first radish I ever grew and its delicious flavor.

At seven, I started my first collection of plants and it was at this point that I met for the first time the *Alocasia cuprea* (elephant's ear), for example, which seemed to me then, as it still does, truly miraculous.

Some years later my father, knowing my tastes, enabled me to take out a subscription to a magazine about plants cultivated in Europe; and this gave me valuable information about plants which could not grow in tropical climates. Other magazines came to my hands, among them *Gartenschönheit,* which was edited by Camillo Schneider and Karl Foerster. The latter is still alive, an authority on everything concerned with the cultivation of plants, but particularly, delphiniums, which he has introduced from many climates similar to that of Germany. It was these early experiences which laid down the direction of my life.

The indigenous plants of Brazil–which were not to be seen in the gardens of Rio de Janeiro–I discovered instead in the hothouses of the Berlin-Dahlem Botanical Garden; and it was frequent visits there that awakened in me the desire to know our flora.

Brazil exists between latitudes, which, with its enormous size, allow the existence of species more numerous than anywhere else

in the world. Its varied configuration, and the number of what we
might call microclimates, enables us to grow plants of very different
environments.

The regions can be divided in this way. There are the forests
of the Amazon, particularly rich in Araceae, *Heliconia,* and huge trees.
In the Cerrados,[1] there are *voquisias, kiemeiras,* and numberless
Leguminosae; an enormous number of trees with twisted trunks
and hairy leaves; and trees that resemble bonsai, whose strange forms
show a long history of adaptation to the particular ecological
conditions of their surroundings, and whose cultivation is a problem
still insufficiently solved. In the Caatinga,[2] there is an infinite number
of Xerophiles, Cactaceas, Mimosaceae, and Euphorbiaceae. On the
cliffs and in the rooks of the mountains, *Vellozias, Barbacenia,* palms,
and *Bromelia* thrive in their natural habitat, as though in miniature
botanical gardens. In the damp forest around the coast, there are
Araceae, Orchidaceae, *Bromelia,* and palms.

There are still other zones such as the Pantanal,[3] the swamps
and marshes of Mato Grosso, where the fields from time to time find
themselves transformed into lakes. This is only a brief outline of a
picture very well painted by Carl Friedrich Philipp von Martius.

So, inspired by the work of Adolf Engler, who constructed the
different groups of flowers in the Berlin-Dahlem Botanical Garden,
I made my first ecological grouping and laid down lines along which
I have traveled ever since, in many different fields of work.

As there was a total lack of good cultivators in Brazil, I was obliged
to cultivate the plants myself. There was a constant interest in the
discovery of worlds completely unknown to me, where the processes
of being born, living, and dying constituted a whole expression of the
determinism of life. All these phases were marked by a kind of beauty
inherent in them and were also linked to all the other processes of
growing in the rest of the world.

My experience is valid principally for Brazil, where each excursion
is still an adventure, but where the satisfaction of discovery completely
compensates for any risk that may have been taken.

I can remember, for instance, a journey across the Amazonian
igapó,[4] where islands of vegetation floated over the calm waters as

though they were houses built on rafts. It is a region where the frequent movement of the waters create a temporary world adapted to its own transitoriness.[5]

On several occasions I traveled through zones where the trees still had the dimensions of trees, but whose trunks were submerged to a distance of 35 feet (10 meters); and generally, in the branches of those trees, was to be found an accumulation of *Bromelia,* Araceae, and even animals.

All the time, one is aware that life is a struggle and feels how marvelous it is that nature should have discovered an equilibrium. From these excursions, I brought back *Heliconia* and a great number of Araceae that became the basis of my specialized collection, considered now the richest in species in the world.

And if, today, I have this collection, I owe it in part to having lived among botanists. I am the friend of many botanists, some of whom are already dead–Adolpho Ducke, João Geraldo Kuhlmann, and Henrique Lahmeyer de Mello Barreto; but others who are still my friends are Correia Gomes, Aparicio Pereira, Graziela Barroso, and Luiz Emygdio. All have helped to enrich my collection, partly by making excursions– all of which were vivid experiences, some of which contained situations of true drama.

In this living together, we established an exchange of impressions and knowledge; and on many occasions we were able to reach conclusions which gave an understanding to the web of mysteries that is nature unaltered by the hand of man; many of those mysteries remain unpenetrated. A research project that still needs to be undertaken is the discovery of the links in the chain that connect the pollination of plants by hummingbirds, insects and their larva, and other elements of animal life in the inflorescences of these plants.[6] Even if we did not always arrive at perfect comprehension, there was always the intention to understand another way of life, through elements like color, volume, rhythm, and movement.

It was only through this kind of experience that I was able to reach an understanding of plants in their habitat and to know that it was not merely an accident that one plant was covered with hair and another opened at night.

The origin of my collection arose from the use of *Heliconia psittacorum* in the Public Garden of Casa Forte in Pernambuco, which I designed in 1935. Later, on account of another species–*Heliconia stricta,* introduced by Jacques Huber to the garden of Museu Goeldi and described by him–I became the friend of the botanist Luiz Emygdio. Another plant, *Heliconia latispatha,* was given to me by the botanist Mello Barreto, who had grown it at Belo Horizonte. At that altitude it had never bloomed; but transported to Rio de Janeiro, it started to flower every year.

My collection has been increased by various excursions, exchanges, purchases, and gifts, and by collecting them personally. At the moment I have, more or less, a hundred listed species. And observation of the *Heliconia* uncovers a work of nature whose constant theme is an enormous richness of solutions and variation. Some pendent ones are covered with what seems to be a kind of wax, resulting in unexpected textures. Sometimes they seem to me almost musical in their harmonies; sometimes they appear to be sculptured volumes detached from space, deep contrasts in their forms being given by the opposition of the flowers to the leaves. Sometimes I have the impression of a painting in their coloration and capriciousness of form. I have seen them in the sun, or during rain, where gradations of light gave them the qualities of precious stones. Sometimes, they are shaped like birds (*Heliconia imbricata*); sometimes like parrotbill (*Heliconia rostrata*) or animals, like *Heliconia mariae,* which has articulated segments like a centipede. Sometimes they have the jeweled quality of a hummingbird, like *Heliconia angustifolia;* or they look like a flight of green birds, like *Heliconia sampaioana. Heliconia amazonica* has the grace of an Impressionist painting–pendent, balanced in the wind under a cinnabar red throat, with bracts that are pink, magenta, green, and white in a tonal sequence never before produced in nature. This spectacle is completed by foliage which seems to have been deliberately cut, a wig raggedly chopped like a rug.

There are *Heliconia* in which the bracts take on an extreme suppleness. They all have the shape of a chalice in order to protect the flowers. Sometimes they are red, or orange-red with mutations to green, dark green, finishing in a clear section that is almost white.

And in the interior, a detached cadmium yellow contrasts with blue
ultramarine fruits, which seem to be emerging from an urn.[7]

In my constant search for plants with new forms, I have been through
some extraordinary moments. On one journey, to Espírito Santo,
I found myself in the Pancas Valley, and was struck by the very definite
character of the region, a series of conical mountains rising out of a
flat plain, across which a river wound like a snake. *Gynerium sagittatum*
(a vigorous, very tall wild grass) formed islands on the plain, the
flowers waving in the wind. But it was in this region that I met a most
important collection of fat, hairy rook plants, and retaining reserves
for unfavorable seasons, some anchored in clefts between the rooks,
forming one of the most beautiful associations I have ever seen.
Here, too, I found Velloziaceae which had adapted themselves to
the variations in season and humidity, sometimes losing their green
and becoming yellow; or, with the coming of rain, turning an intense
and luminous green; then finally producing a flower of such beauty
that Martius called it *lírio-da-montanha,* or mountain lily (*Vellozia
candida*).

It was journeys like this which gave me a more thorough
understanding of plants in their habitat, and of the right way in which
to associate them. Many times I have placed together plants
which, though coming from different regions, had a close similarity,
a brotherhood, in their needs and attitudes.

In these journeys in search of the unknown, as we arrived at the
wonder that is the discovery of the plant, with all its novelty, the revelation
of form and color reached paroxysm, a sudden outburst of emotion.[8]
There were times, of course, at which one seemed to approach death,
as on one occasion, on a journey to Espírito Santo, when I nearly
slipped down a cliff trying to collect a plant that I wanted. Or it would
be an accident caused by the bad roads in some primitive part of
the country.

Once we took up a hitchhiker to whom I involuntarily, and in a
joke, attributed the evil eye. In consequence, from that moment, there
were a number of unaccountable accidents. Our driver hit a man in
Vitória, scalping him. Luckily, he didn't die, but it complicated our lives
very much. A little later, all four tires were punctured. Farther on, near

a little village, our station wagon skidded down the hillside; and, before
we had recovered from this, a petrol tanker truck crashed into us.
I felt particularly close to death on this occasion, as the local inhabitants,
searching for us in the dark, did so with lighted matches. To crown
the situation, our driver and one of the men started to fight with each
other and a stabbing was narrowly avoided; and later, one of the
men was attacked by a jarraracussu, a very poisonous snake. In spite
of all of this, however, we collected material of a superlative quality,
including a palm tree that, according to the botanist Aparicio Pereira,
is of a species not yet described.[9]

I want to try and tell you about the almost violent attraction that
these journeys in search of new plants have for me. It is as if the forest
offered treasure only to those who go in search of it, and I feel every
day how short my life is to know and explore all the treasures of the
Brazilian flora. It is a situation simply described as *un embarras de
richesse,* "an embarrassment of riches."[10] Colors repeat themselves
in different tones, and the forms organize themselves into long series,
each theme subjected to an infinity of variations. Many times we
find that the principal interest is the analogous nature of the relationships,
the complementary nature of their characters—as, for instance,
in the case of *Tibouchina granulosa* (a tree with purple flowers) and the
Chorisia (silk floss tree),[11] or the *Vochysia,* whose old gold color
finds an exact correspondence in the color of the *Jussieua* (water
primrose). Sometimes, this resemblance extends beyond the vegetable,
into the animal world. The bright red of the Mulungus, a tree with a
very beautiful flower, repeats itself exactly in the color of birds like the
sangue-de-bois. At other times, the similarity of forms—in reality,
simply an expression of the laws of symmetry and growth which plants
obey—can associate beings extremely remote from each other in the
phylogenetic series—as, for instance, the flower of the *Costus,* whose
helical bracts remind one of the fruits of a conifer.

I think that the study of form in its multiple planes, from the
molecular to the megascopic, would be an indispensable factor in
any new formulation of the problem of the philosophy of nature. Inside
this field of observation, and from the study of form, there exist
ecological solutions that can express clearly how life resolves its

problems of form in relation to function. For instance, the sight of a *Ceiba erianthos* cramming its huge roots into a very small portion of soil is equilibrium in disequilibrium. And what can one say of the *Meriania,* with branches in the form of swollen fingers whose function it is to store food and water for the difficult times. Then there is a *Cephalocereus fluminensis,* which slides over rocks like a hairy snake, but in the appropriate season opens in a rapid and magnificent flowering, a prelude to the formation of the seed that perpetuates life.

To understand plants or their forms it is necessary to understand all of the series of profiles that define a plant in time and space. Analyzing it, one can find a succession of necessary states, complementary and interdependent–germination, growing, flowering, and fruiting–phenomena which translate a position in space into a projection in time. One needs to understand that there is a profound reason for the *Cassia* to flower together in a certain time. The *Erythrina* does the same. There seems almost to be a conspiracy in this simultaneous flowering. They are like a series of chromatic chords, during each one of which Nature dresses herself as for a festival.

All of the experience I acquired while traveling, in so many years of work, induced me to try to understand nature, both in surface and in depth. I have been preoccupied with the richness manifested by the flora of my own country. The strangest adaptations that one can find are there. Color, form, and function create rhythm, a rhythm that expresses life. I have tried to apply this rhythm to my gardens; without it, I could never have achieved in depth the creative capacity to which I have aspired.

But one must never forget that these elements should be used by the landscape architect as elements in a composition. They should be used following the laws and principles that are valid for any work of art–gardens must be composed as works of art. One must decide what is to be said, and how; and it should be expressed in a neat, clear, and legible way.

One can use repetitions, analogies, contrasts, approximations, and spaces–relations of volumes, surfaces, and lines–and one can also relate form, color, and texture.

The onlooker must be conducted through these elements in such a way that he feels himself inside a unity, as the richness of detail reveals itself as in music, space, and time. In landscape architecture, one cannot possibly speak of aesthetics in any isolated way.[12] Gardens are linked with all the functions that exist in nature to form an organic unity; and also bound up in it are the lives of human beings, in search of equilibrium, happiness, or identification with their surroundings. This sense of communion shows itself in the many small nuances that can awake poetic feelings; and these feelings of pleasure, or the awareness of beauty, with those even of simply feeling hot or cold, come down to the physical and chemical processes which are the basis of all vital manifestations.

To conclude, I should like to say that all of the gardens I have created are the result of the experiences I have related to you. All of my efforts have been directed toward avoiding the fruit of a routine composition or of any aesthetic preconception.

I aspire toward a completely free creation, although it must be rooted deeply in my understanding of nature and of the world; and this understanding is given light and depth by two very important sentiments, those which formed the pattern of the life of Saint Francis of Assisi: the love that directs us and the humility that corrects us.

Original text used for comparing the translation: Roberto Burle Marx, "Depoimento pessoal," in *Arte e paisagem: conferências escolhidas,* ed. José Tabacow (São Paulo: Nobel, 2004), 15–21.

1   Cerrado is the savanna region in central Brazil, accounting for more than 20 percent of the land area of Brazil.

2   Caatinga is one of the Brazilian ecoregions, characterized by small thorny trees and shrubland.

3   The Pantanal is a tropical wetland region in Brazil.

4   Igapó is a term used in Brazil to describe freshwater-flooded forests in the Amazon region, which are either flooded permanently or seasonally.

5   Original: *transitoriedade.*

6   "A research project that still needs to be undertaken…the inflorescences of these plants" is present in the English translation but absent from the Portuguese edition.

7   "The origin of my collection…which seem to be emerging from an urn" is present in the English translation but absent from the Portuguese edition.

8   "In these journeys…of form and color reached paroxysm" is present in the Portuguese edition but absent from the English translation.

9   "Once we took up a hitchhiker… a species not yet described" is present in the English translation but absent from the Portuguese edition.

10 This phrase was in French in the Portuguese edition.

11 The taxonomic genus *Chorisia* has been folded into *Ceiba.*

12 Original: *paisagismo.*

The Function of the Garden

Undated Portuguese lecture. Translated into English by Celina Engersen, 1970, Rio de Janeiro. An unverified handwritten note indicates that the lecture was delivered at Harvard University.

To speak of gardens is always difficult and complex, for every composition follows a logical pattern, as well as predetermined principles that cannot be wholly explained in so many words. Yet when I try to define, to bring out a clean-cut idea, I strive to present the reasons that move me toward my composition.

At first when I began to work, in my eagerness to express myself, the ideas tumbled out: they overlapped and the motive was to express everything in mind within the same garden. Today, after so many years, one goes through very marked changes, especially changes of form, of rhythm, of color, and the concept of use sometimes prevails over all of the others. To make a synthesis, to say the maximum one can say with a minimum of means, is difficult; and that is why I admire Matisse who, in an effort to reach a synthesis, goes gradually through a series of eliminations, retaining the essential while succeeding in concealing his craftsmanship. I believe in the initial impulse when kept restrained so that, when the composition is ready, no reductions or additions are required.

When it comes to gardens, there is no doubt that it is through them that we can get some relief in a life so full of ups and downs in our industrial civilization. I am convinced that the community garden, square, or park will have an ever-growing importance in our lives, in our quest for an acceptable balance within the instability of the present civilization. The garden will have a social as well as an educational and scientific character, where its functions will be determined by the aspirations of an era, linked to man's aesthetic and ethical conduct. Today, no one would create a garden like Versailles, where the central figure was the Sun King, supreme in his conscious absolutism, and who succeeded in unifying France politically and dominating a number of smaller states, imposing French prestige in Europe. This does not prevent us from recognizing that the important thing, besides the other functions that it served, was the significant sense of change that the landscape underwent, when it was arranged in orderly, well-defined groups, based on aesthetic directives, carrying out this highly important interplay of volumes in relation to calm surfaces, establishing contrasts by means of textures and opposing materials, and where the pieces of sculpture unfold in a rhythmic pattern. The water, besides reflecting the sky and the environment, with its *jeux-d'eau* (water play) creates spaces and images; and the clearings establish a contrast with the woodland.[1] It is a geometrization of nature or of the landscape, based on the aesthetic necessity of developing relationships and proportions, all of which are coherent with the dominating rationalism of French philosophy of the time.

There are some principles that guide us; they must not, however, be mistaken for formulas. Each composition has to exist in function with the way of living; the area; the peculiarities of each case; its utilization and its climate. The Japanese were fully aware of this when they tried to express a state of mind by means of a proposed composition. Thus, a garden made for a warrior cannot be the same as the one for a priest who sits in meditation and seeks isolation from the external world.

The city garden, whether it is a garden planned for a school, an industrial plant, or a hospital, assumes a greater significance because it is closely linked to the urban question. Even large parking lots should be given a garden landscape solution, so as to reinstate the city dweller—a prisoner in areas of the most pressing activities—in a more dignified setting.

When I speak of city gardens I also have in mind squares, which are closely related to architecture, the relationship of man and his highly diversified activities. While thinking in terms of modern city planning, one great concern should be to guarantee the preservation of green areas, allowing the city dweller contact with nature, and not leading him to feel lost in a mass of concrete that little by little takes possession of the scanty free space still left in large cities.

Large cities are becoming more and more inhuman. Air pollution, lack of green areas, and haphazard city growth without any planning have all contributed to the misunderstanding of what an ideal city could be, with its woodland, picnic sites, playing fields, open-air theaters; with open spaces where people could meet or make use of swimming pools; and above all, where the imagination would contribute toward the aesthetic aspects so necessary in our daily life.

After all of the years I have devoted to the art of making gardens,
I am convinced that the plant itself performs an outstanding role
in most cases, and that without a thorough knowledge of them it is
impossible to compose a garden.[2] In Brazil, where the flora is so
generously rich, we have a wide vocabulary at our disposal.
Unfortunately, because of lack of knowledge, the vocabulary is little
used and cultivated. I can firmly say, however, that some juxtaposition
of plants, some associations and massing of similar ecological
groups, form completely new expressions from the point of view of
garden landscapes.[3] It is curious to observe that the wide use of plants
of different kinds was, above all, the work of naturalists, botanists,
and collectors of the 19th century. At present, there is, especially in
my country, a conventional preestablished vocabulary that is
almost always the same, resulting many times in a disturbing monotony.
Such gardens could be either in Venezuela, or in The Bahamas,
or anywhere, for no consideration is taken of the inherent ecological
characteristics of each case. It is a conventional vocabulary, employed
internationally, where sentimentalism is expressed through plants
from incompatible climates, resulting in an unsatisfactory growth. Thus
the necessity of problem-solving, which, when well guided, would
bring surprisingly enchanting results by valuing the aesthetic of the local
or imported flora, under the criteria of ecological balance.

While traveling throughout Brazil, I have come across plants that
could be employed in the most varied climates: plants that grow well
in swamps and lakes, and others that withstand the sea air and the
highly saturated saline soil, plants that cover the plains, and others that
grow on the slopes of the mountains and at the feet of the hills.

There are combinations that are extraordinarily interesting and
attractive. Vegetation, for instance, that shoots up from iron ore rocks on
the granite gneiss cliffs or in the crevices and layers of limestone rocks.

There are plants that can live through long droughts, such as
the flora of the cattle-grazing land around Brasília, or of the Caatinga,
a stunted, spare forest in northeastern Brazil, where thorny plants,
like cacti, are characteristic.

When we understand a region ecologically, we can employ a vast
number of plants never previously put to use.

Of course, endless research would be necessary to ascertain the adaptation of certain species. Many of them grow attached to micro-roots, without which they could not live. I am convinced that once they are biologically understood, following scientific study, many plants that until now have not been adopted will be a welcome challenge in planning new gardens.

No plant lives in isolation but in relation to others, and it is only by means of comparison, by establishing the relationships, the analogy of forms, or by their contrasts, that we many times can bring certain qualities into evidence.

As far as I am concerned there are no ugly plants. There are, rather, plants that go with one another and plants that do not harmonize. As for their use, the ecological aspect is much more important than any other in their association. In a forest of sequoias, it would be horrible to see banana trees growing, just as it would be horrible to see the cedars of Lebanon growing in a tropical forest full of epiphytes.

There is an intrinsic expression peculiar to each region and this should be borne in mind. I am afraid that, in the future, many plants that are yet to be used in our country may disappear, thanks to some profit-minded individuals and to the ignorance of others that destroy them unwittingly.

Under these circumstances, the importance of gardens in our daily life increases. I recently journeyed to the north of Brazil, where there are trees that stand 180 feet (55 meters) high and where there is an immense wealth of botanical species. And yet, whoever undertakes an expedition through these regions will end up bitter and annoyed, for not only is the land scarred by the lane cut by the road builders, but also along the embankment, on both sides, all growth is burnt away in a most brutal form.

If a museum were to suffer damage from fire, the whole of humanity would regret the loss. And yet millions of trees, some more than 500 years old, are destroyed amid general indifference. I should like to caution all those who are not aware of what is taking place, and say that we are destroying a heritage that belongs not only to us but also to future generations.[4]

A garden cannot be made solely with hybrids and half a dozen trees that adapt themselves easily. **It is our duty to respect what we have and perpetuate, by means of seed collections, nurseries, transplanting of seedlings, grafting, layering, etc.** All of this remaining flora that challenges us calls for a more intelligent utilization, so as to provide us with an aesthetic and ethical sense of existence. If we so act, we shall have at our disposal an extremely rich flora, and all we have to do is preserve it.

It is man himself who, out of ignorance, has been destroying for thousands of years these riches granted to him. If we do not think immediately about giving those who will follow us a better life, humanity will survive deprived of its original nature.

If we base ourselves on the laws of composition, where there is a play of volumes, of rhythms, a contrast and harmony of forms, the employment of colors, understanding at the same time that the plants go through vegetative cycles of instability; and if we take these mutations into consideration, plus the cycle of the days, from sunrise to sunset, passing through the wide spectrum of changes; and if at night we make use of electricity in a less vulgar and aggressive manner; and if we further take into consideration the sounds, the rippling of the waters, the rustlings of the wind on the treetops, the fragrances characteristic of every season; and if, above all, we accept the existence of certain species, **not losing sight of all sociological implications,** then we shall, through our effort, have guaranteed a life better balanced and more equitable for man in the industrial civilization.

Original text used for comparing the translation: Roberto Burle Marx, "A função do jardim," in *Arte e paisagem: conferências escolhidas,* ed. José Tabacow (São Paulo: Nobel, 2004), 207–13.

1   In the Portuguese edition, the phrase is in French: *jeux d'eau.*
2   Original: ... *é difícil compor.*
3   Original: ... *vista jardinístico.*
4   Original: ... *um legado que não pertence apenas a nós, mas às gerações vindouras.*

Finding a Garden Style to Meet Contemporary Needs

This lecture was delivered in English at Harvard University Graduate School of Design at an unverified date. The lecture has Burle Marx's handwritten annotations, many of which have been incorporated into this edited text. Original editing possibly by Mario Romanach of Burle Marx & Cia Ltda. The text is based on a 1954 essay in *Landscape Architecture Magazine,* Roberto Burle Marx, "A Garden Style in Brazil to Meet Contemporary Needs: With Emphasis on the Paramount Value of Native Plants," *Landscape Architecture* 44, no. 4 (1954): 200-08. http://www.jstor.org/stable/44659298.

It may seem strange to you that a landscape architect from the tropics should come to propose to you, who live in a country with northern traditions and a northern climate, solutions which, in the past 20 years, he has been seeking for gardens in Brazil.[1]

Yet these experiments have interested landscape artists and architects who do not work in the tropics, just as it seems that Brazilian contemporary architecture has suggested solutions adopted sometimes successfully but sometimes less so by architects in quite different climates and under differing social conditions. The garden I designed for Mrs. Tremayne in Santa Barbara, California, with flora suitable to Santa Barbara, was never laid out,[2] but the colored chart for this garden was exhibited at your university and is a permanent exhibit in the Museum of Modern Art in New York; and it has brought me many letters that suggested that people all over the world are seeking solutions to a problem identical with my own–that of finding a garden style to meet contemporary needs–artistic, social, and economic, for the man in the city as well as the country dweller. Ten years ago, in *Brazil Builds: Architecture New and Old, 1652–1942,* Philip Goodwin published some of these solutions,[3] made in collaboration with our new generation of architects, inspired by Le Corbusier's visit to Brazil:[4] and an article which appeared in *Architectural Review* in 1947 suggested that "once the idea of the contemporary garden, planned according to Burle Marx's principles, has been postulated, its variations need have no limits."[5]

What these simple basic principles are, and how I have carried them out in a tropical climate, is what I hope to illustrate during the course of this talk.

But first of all, what does a landscape architect like myself understand by a garden?[6] There are many public squares with beaten earth and a few unpainted benches and one or two old trees which as of yet have not been uprooted, which are still called gardens, but are not worthy of the name.

A garden in its wider sense is, I think, a careful selection of certain aspects of nature: water, rock, flower, and foliage; ordered and arranged by man; and in which man may have direct contact with plants. An area in space, however small, in which he may find rest, relaxation, recreation, and above all the feeling that he is living in, and integrated into, this space. It is also a complex of plastic intentions, with a utilitarian purpose: and it should, whenever possible, fuse with the surrounding landscape, while being an extension of the architecture for which it is designed.

For instance, it may be a roof garden where workers in the office building can spend their lunch hour, a collective garden for an apartment building—and in this case it should be planted with hardy sculptural plants, in order to withstand exposure to strong winds, and in order to complete the architecture with smaller but decorative contrasting volumes. If, in the case of a public square, it is not designed to be the continuation of the architecture, then it should have architectural characteristics of its own—say, an acoustic shell for music, attractively designed benches for those who sit there, a mosaic-faced pool, or a pool backed by a wall with a mural—something to arrest the interest, and create pleasure and surprise. But above all, it is a place in which the plant is the dominant element, chosen and placed not mechanically and according to a standard specification, but in such a way as to produce constant exaltation in the visitor. I stress this point because so much importance has been given lately (and understandably) to constructional materials (wood, concrete flower boxes, and so on) which simplify the general upkeep and reduce staff costs of gardeners both in private and public gardens, that the plant, the chief actor in the spectacle, is gradually being imprisoned on smaller and smaller stages, and the feeling of growth, of pulsating life, is being stifled. This does not mean that the freestanding wall faced with mosaic or blue glaze tiles, which I use for privacy or windbreaks as well as with aesthetic intention, or the granite or stone slabs used for paths, benches, and sculptural elements, do not have their legitimate place in the contemporary garden—but anyone who has stood in the shade of a constructed wall, looking out onto the garden, and then has moved to the cooler shadow of an overhanging tree, knows the immense physical and aesthetic difference. There is life in the shade of a living tree, life in the colors and shapes one perceives, under its protection.

Then, too, a garden is man's conception of nature as she presents herself to us. In England, where much of the so-called natural scenery is a legacy of the brilliant landscape gardening of the 18th century, this statement may not seem entirely accurate; but in Brazil–where even today in unexplored regions, man is fighting a hostile nature, cutting and burning before he replants–the jungle has little similarity with a garden. It is true that nature has her own sharply defined laws, which tell of a close interrelation between trees, plants, animals, birds, and insects. In the Amazon basin there are parrot-hued *Heliconia* with bracts which might as well be parrot's beaks,[7] both as regards their color and structure; there are grasshoppers which might be leaves in the wind; butterflies which might be orchids; orchids which might be butterflies. Once I unwillingly witnessed a hunt for little green parakeets. When the birds fell to the ground, the soil seemed strewn, not with dead green birds, but with living green leaves. And though there exists an interdependence in nature, there is also a constant fight going on, one plant or animal striving to survive, to assert itself, at the cost of weaker elements. Whereas in a garden, it is the landscape architect who decides which shall be the dominant plant, at least in the period of creation and execution.

Of course, he may decide, for some definite demonstrational or didactic purpose, to reproduce in miniature some plant or animal life complex, depicting as faithfully as possible, nature in her original state. That is just what I did, in collaboration with the great botanist Henrique Lahmeyer de Mello Barreto, now head of the Federal District's Zoological Garden. We reproduced one section of a park designed to be a prototype of the vegetation and bird and animal habitats of the Federal District–the home of marsh birds. We had the wonderful experience of finding that, in this habitat, not only did the plants and the birds both thrive wonderfully, but also other wild marsh birds, whose homes are vanishing as the marshland is being reclaimed, had flown in from far off, and joined the colony! Such an experiment is, however, both impossibly expensive (not even in the Zoological Gardens could we carry out the entire project) and, in addition, the island was planned for the birds and for scientific experiment more than for human beings.

The planning of a garden must take into account the purpose for which it is being designed, as well as the location. Obviously in the marsh bird complex I mentioned, no cacti would be planted, nor would one put a rosebush at the edge of a pool devoted to the *Victoria regia* (water lily). The size, the shape, the chief characteristics, and the proportion of plants in relation to constructional elements will depend on the sort of people who are going to use the garden. A children's garden, such as the one at Pedregulho Housing Complex in Rio de Janeiro designed by Affonso Eduardo Reidy, will need sand, areas where recreational equipment may be placed, and plants hardy enough to stand up to rough usage. A garden for old people will need benches strategically placed in sun and shade, with elements of higher aesthetic interest: water pools, mosaic paths, tiled wall murals, fountains, or statuary. And a lovers' garden, such as I designed for the recreation island in Rodrigo de Freitas Lagoon, in Rio de Janeiro, should have a slightly private atmosphere, achieved by the planting of arbors facing the lake. There are, however, no hard or fast rules, no formulas for common sense, and each new problem is a challenge to the creative impulse of the landscape architect, each one demanding an authentically different solution.[8] I do not believe in the standardized garden—and in any case the plants themselves, living personalities reacting differently to similar conditions, will see to it that no two gardens, even if they have been prepared to specification, will turn out exactly alike.

But if there are no hard and fast rules, I suspect that the general principles on which a garden may be constructed differ very little whether the garden is being designed for Boston or Brazil. In any environment, a garden should be designed according to existing topography,[9] and planted in accordance with the climatic and soil conditions of the region. In other words, the garden that has the best chances of survival and needs the minimum amount of care for such survival will be indigenous. This sounds like a very obvious statement, but evidence proves the contrary. Today, when labor is at a premium, when practically no one, even in Brazil, can afford a full-time gardener, when municipal gardeners are an infinitesimal proportion of city employees, the problem of upkeep as well as layout is a primary consideration. The indigenous Brazilian plant requires infinitely less care than the average imported plant—and moreover, the foliage plants in my country are perennials.

Especially if they are logically located–the shade plants under the canopies of trees (but not under pilotis, where they do not do well) and the sun-loving plants in beds right out in the open–these components of the "Brazilian garden" will be more economical and far more attractive than that of an "imported" one, where the plants, which are so beautiful in such cooler climates as yours, have to struggle to stay alive–and show the signs of this struggle.

This is no chauvinistic point of view, no desire to exclude plants from other countries. Although we know that the Brazilian flora is one of the richest and most surprising in the world, our plant vocabulary for gardens, up to the first quarter of this century, was exceedingly small. Whereas certain plants and trees, imported less than 150 years ago, have in many cases established themselves here so firmly that they have become integrated into the landscape, and appear to be Brazilian. The best example of this is the imperial palm (*Roystonea oleracea*), which was brought to Brazil in 1808, by order of Dom João VI, and planted in the Botanical Garden of Rio de Janeiro which he inaugurated in that year.[10] Those who know the great architectural colonnades of this palm, in these gardens, along the avenue lining the lake of the Ministry of Foreign Affairs in Brasília, or the other avenue following the Flamengo Beach leading to the South Zone of Rio, rarely, if ever, remember that this palm is not indigenous, and that it was a Portuguese monarch who had it brought from the Antilles. But as the climate is similar, it thrives here, and grows to a height of over 100 feet (30 meters). All living examples of the species in Brazil are the children of one great mother, still alive in the Rio Botanical Gardens. It is my plan to use this palm, not in a single avenue, but in massed phalanxes forming an architectural colonnade, an orderly comparison with the "chaos" of the tropical forest. On the municipality's recreation island in the Rodrigo de Freitas Lagoon, two of these colonnades, geometrically planted, were designed to flank the baroque of an Oscar Niemeyer restaurant and boat club, linked together by an avenue of equally tall trees, the *pau-mulato (Calycophyllum spruceanum)* from the Amazon, which has a smooth, slender trunk going through many shades of color from coffee brown, to orange, to lettuce green, at different seasons of the year.

The poverty of the cultivated plant vocabulary in Brazil is due partly
to the fact that the Amerindian's habit was to burn down forest and
plant only those foods or medicinal elements essential to his existence.
He planted many kinds of maize, from white and green to yellow and
almost dark brown. Brazilian plants found in early gardens are mostly
due to the Franciscan monks who planted them in their cloister patios,
in the north especially. What we find in the oldest gardens we know are
the *manacá* with its white lilac and deep purple flowers all growing
on the same bush, the *pitangueira* tree with its tiny red pumpkin fruit,
the ipê tree with its golden bunches of flowers lighting up forest
hillsides as well as gardens, the deep purple *quaresmeira,* and the
elaborate pink flowers of the *Musa rosacea.* The roses, violets,
and pansies in these old gardens—especially the ones high up above Rio
de Janeiro in the Tijuca forest—were brought to Brazil by Europeans
from Portugal, England, and France, who came on business, or to the
Imperial Court. Other indigenous plants were planted for medicinal,
nutritional, or aromatic purposes. For compensation many plants were
taken from Brazil back to Europe by both visitors and botanists, such
as Augustin Saint-Hilaire and Carl Friedrich Philipp von Martius. In
Europe the plants were met by a vogue for the exotic, which reached
its height at the end of the 19th century. A number of hybrids of such
plants were produced in Europe and unknown in Brazil: orchids and
Gloxinia, Verbena, Salvia, Justicia and *Philodendron,* and *Anthurium*
were all better known in Europe than to our fathers.

When we find a gap in our plant vocabulary, and this gap can be filled
by an imported exotic plant that harmonizes with the landscape,
I think that this plant should be used. The deep violet of the *Hemigraphis
colorata* (flame ivy), the purple and green-gray sword blades of
the Mexican *Rhoeo discolor* (boat lily), and a whole legion of Venetian-red
Acalypha (copperleaf) are indispensable to the landscape architect's
palette,[11] and were easily acclimatized. In the Botafogo Parkway, which
links the southern zone of Copacabana to the rest of the city, I used
non-Brazilian plants side by side with indigenous ones. Their brilliant
colors or sculptural forms helped to catch the eye of the motorist
speeding by, planted as they were in beds with fluid shapes, symbolizing
movement to the spectator.

One way to fill the gaps in the plant vocabulary is to hybridize. Now, my Pernambucan mother,[12] whose grandparents had grown English gardens in Apipucos (a suburb of Recife, the capital of Pernambuco state) with imported English plants, but also with indigenous trees, was herself an enthusiastic cultivator of Brazilian plants, such as the *tinhorão* (*Caladium bicolor*) with its stained glass window leaves, through which life pulsates in whites, pinks, and reds. I too learned to hybridize them, and I once obtained a very rare purple tone. Each new shape or tone created is always a source of delight, because the new tone will give one new possibilities of composition.

The results obtained with the *tinhorão* impressed Lúcio Costa, the true father of contemporary Brazilian architecture,[13] when he visited our garden in Leme in Rio de Janeiro in 1932 and saw a flower bed I had planted with white *tinhorãos* and deep purple-brown coleus foliage. He decided that the painter I was then studying to become–under Candido Portinari, after having studied with Leo Putz–should have a chance to be a landscape architect of the new style.[14] He commissioned me to design the garden for the house he and Gregori Warchavchik,[15] recently arrived in Brazil, had built and were putting on exhibition in Copacabana.[16] Nothing remains of the house or garden today, 20 years later–but this gave me my chance.

Later, the city of Recife invited me in 1934 to lay out three important municipal gardens. Into the designing of these I put everything I knew. I believed then, as I believe now, that a water garden, especially in a climate like ours, is an essential element, whether it is used as a life-giving parterre, as a fountain sculpture, or as a mirror. So I made a three-pooled water garden for the historical square of the Casa Forte– and in the central circular pool, for the first time in Brazil, I planted our *Victoria regia,* a water lily with leaves 6 feet (2 meters) in diameter, and in the two rectangular pools flanking it, I grew indigenous aquatic plants in one and exotics in the other. I was inspired by pictures in the splendid review dedicated to gardens, *Gartenschönheit,* which had shown me many aspects of Kew Gardens.

Another garden at some distance from this one, situated in the Benfica district, was inspired by an ecological garden I had seen in the Berlin-Dahlem Botanical Garden–a cactus garden in which many

species with their strange forms and brilliant colors grew. The great
majority of the cacti came from the states of Bahia and Pernambuco,
but which I had never seen until I went to Germany. Although the gardens
have changed a great deal since I finished them in 1937, it is still
possible to discern that in these, my first, I used geometric, symmetrical,
classical forms for the water gardens (as at Kew, and also long ago
in China). But in the case of the ecological garden, it was not only more
effective but far more practical to use free forms—and this garden is the
one which has survived the best.

This type of garden, despite the interest it has maintained over
time, was met with opposition in 1937, as well as with praise—for public
gardens at that time were a perfect example of European homesickness,
with geometrical flower beds and terrible topiary, that would have
drawn a laugh from Francis Bacon himself (he compared topiary shapes
to pies). These were gardens a very long time after André Le Nôtre.[17]
While in Copacabana the bungalow gardens grew sickly firs and pines,
copied out of *House and Garden,* but providing positive proof that they
were unsuited to a tropical climate. These puny styles were inadequate
against the dramatic outlines of the Rio mountains, with their steep
gray rocks, thickly wooded at the foot, and their miniature Sugar Loaf
repeated across the Guanabara Bay; while their colors became pale
in comparison with the orange-red soil that is deep pink and even purple
at the core.

One public garden in Rio, however, which is always full of people,
harmonizes with the topography, using wide, sloping lawns, strategically
planted trees for shade and contrast, winding streams with luxuriantly
planted miniature islands, and different textures and hues of green for
ground cover. It always seemed to me when I was a boy, and it seems
to me still, to be essentially Brazilian, essentially satisfactory as a Rio
public garden: and the fact that it is constantly used is a proof of its
success. It is planted on the site of Rio's first public garden, made by
silversmith Frei Valentim in 1773, on what had been a marsh, but
was ordered to be filled in by Viceroy Vasconcellos, by the simple order
of rounding up the "vagabonds and guitar players" and forcing them
to tear down a hill for the purpose! This garden, a series of tree avenues
in the early geometrical style of William Kent, was replanted 90 years

later from the jungle it had become by Auguste François Marie Glaziou, a Breton landscape architect and engineer who came to Brazil from Bordeaux in 1860.

Glaziou's Passeio Público, which seemed so Brazilian to me, was actually the English landscape garden of Kent and Shenstone, as brought to Bagatelle and Trianon by the Prince de Caraman-Chimay. If I mention what must be known to all of you—that this style was a product of the Grand Tour, of Claude Lorrain and Salvator Rosa, of ancient Chinese silk landscapes—it is because through Glaziou (although he also brought blasted tree trunks in concrete, stalagmite grottos, and Swiss châlets), all of these influences have influenced Brazilian gardens, including mine. I admired his sweeping lawns, varied ground-cover texture, use of boulders for creating Rio landscapes by analogy (even though Glaziou's boulders were faced with concrete!), and as a landscape architect I was sure that his weekend jungle trips must have caused him to plant many more Brazilian plants than have survived today, along with *Ravenala madagascariensis* (traveler's palm), *Ficus retusa* (a dark-leaved tree), and others imported through the French firm of Vilmorin and Andrieux. His imports have become part of our landscape, since he was careful to choose from similar climates.

From air journeys I have made over Brazil, I can see as he could not that his winding streams, although inspired by the landscape garden, were also perfect microcosms of the baroque Brazilian rivers. If he had been alive today, I feel sure that he would have experienced, as I have, the sensation of seeing these rivers as abstract arabesques; as, too, the lettuce-green patches of sugarcane fields over which one flies appear to me to be two-dimensional color, which can be reproduced either in a garden, or in a painting abstracted from what originally inspired them. For Glaziou, as his many other landscape gardens prove, may have come to Brazil as a drainage engineer, but he was the true father-artist of our gardens.

Glaziou's influence, and my visit to the Berlin-Dahlem Botanical Garden in 1928, convinced me that one of the important problems to be solved in Brazil was the enrichment of plant colors and vocabulary. Since the municipal nursery gardens and the private nursery gardeners had very little to offer, this meant going into the interior, in search of

aquatic plants, and blue-flowering plants, especially–a color lacking
in our flower scheme. I brought back specimens from the Amazon,
from the states of Espírito Santo and Bahia, and from ecological
expeditions into the rocky mountain deserts of Minas Gerais, with
Henrique Lahmeyer de Mello Barreto. It may be hard for you to
imagine my excitement waiting for seeds to germinate and cuttings to
put forth roots, unless you can imagine first the effort these trips
entailed, because of the lack of transport to these far-off regions. One
great disappointment of mine is that the seeds of the wonderful
cobalt blue flowering tree (*Qualea ingens*) I found blazing in central Brazil
amongst orange-flowering trees, refused to germinate in the less-
acidic Rio soil. It lives in very dangerous country, where sixteen out of
twenty people have caught the terrible Bauru (leishmaniasis) disease,
so it was not easy for me to return there. But the nursery garden I now
have in Campo Grande contains 68 species of *Heliconia* (false bird-
of-paradise), the largest collection in the world; a great number of rare
Philodendron; a varied collection of *Dieffenbachia* (a genus of
flowering plants); and many unclassified water plants, one of which
bears my name, to mention but a few trophies brought back from
these trips. And these are the raw materials with which I work.

In addition to bringing back new plants, I believe we should also use
known but rare ones, such as the Monkey's Apricot or *Couroupita
guianensis,* one example of which grows in Rio Botanical Gardens with
a rose-like flower growing on crooked-finger branches all the way
up the trunk to the top–while other branches only bear leaves. Another
example I have already mentioned; it is the *pau-mulato* (*Calycophyllum
spruceanum*) with its slender coffee to pale green columns. Every
such rare plant suggests to the landscape architect a new manner of
planting. The *Couroupita,* if planted closely in a copse, would give
one an entirely new emotional experience, and the *pau-mulato,* closely
planted, would create some strange, unknown temple.

In a garden, we should also preserve the beautiful wild plants so often
neglected. In the 4th Centennial Gardens designed for Ibirapuera Park,
I had meant to plant a large bed of the characteristic wild flowers of São
Paulo State. We should also rescue forgotten plants from oblivion,
and plants which are being systematically destroyed from disappearing

entirely. Lack of understanding is killing off the unusual Rio seashore vegetation, the "resting," while the stone quarry plants are being ruthlessly torn up to sell in street fairs. So I have planted many of these species in a section of the large park up in the granite mountain district above Petrópolis, and in the sandy section, near the bay, of the Botafogo Parkway. As well, the flora of the Santos Dumont Airport garden is entirely Brazilian so that the visitor to Rio, from the moment of his arrival, can get a sensation of the Federal District habitats. (The great volumes, the trees, are not fully grown as yet, so the true artistic intention cannot yet be sensed.)

This garden has a little lake, to which I attach great importance; for a water garden, in addition to preserving some of the most beautiful specimens of our flora, needs so comparatively little care. The lake is the heart of the garden–and in it grow reeds and marginal plants, which had been entirely neglected. The stone quarry group includes those plants which have had to fight hard for survival, such as the purple *Tibouchina* which has hairy leaves for catching dew; *Ceiba eriodendron,* with its "Lurçat" thorns, developed to protect surprisingly small leaves and ermine-like flowers; the *Clusia fluminensis,* which developed thick leaves to store water. In a sandy section, far to the right of the lake, I have planted the palm which was being uprooted from Rio's sandy beaches, *Acrocomia sclerocarpa.* I have placed curving concrete benches in this garden, so that those who come to sit there can experience something new.

Up to now, I have described to you some of the plants with which I work, and shown you their importance in my gardens. But a garden is a complex of aesthetic and plastic intentions; and the plant is, to a landscape artist, not only a plant, rare, unusual, ordinary or doomed to disappearance–it is also a color, a shape, a volume, or an arabesque in itself. It is the paint for the two-dimensional picture I make of a garden on a drawing board in my atelier, it is the sculpture or arabesque completing the geometric or asymmetrical abstract of a glass mosaic panel on a freestanding wall, which has been constructed not only for privacy but also to create a special atmosphere; it is the shadow which dapples a blue-glaze tile wall that creates depth on a shallow hillside terrace, but is also

a picture seen through the window of a house. And again it is the large
sculptural element contrasted with the soft textures and contours
of a marginal tapestry around a pool–or the tapestry broderie itself, in
abstract designs in a foliage parterre such as one in the garden
belonging to Walter Moreira Salles, who was Brazil's ambassador to
Washington. Or it may be, as in the case of the imperial palms, an
architectural element, representing a limitation of space in an outdoor
house for man.

For it is not only as a botanist and as a working gardener that I think
of gardens. I was trained as a painter, as I have told you, and I worked
under Portinari on the Products of Brazil panels for the Minister of
Education's private office in Rio.[18] The problems of color contrast
and harmony, of structure and form, are as important to
me as a two-dimensional painter as they are to me in the
three-dimensional or four-dimensional garden. My two
professions complement each other.

It seems to me, in fact, that the principles on which I base the
structure and arrangement of my gardens, are in many points identical
to those which are at the root of any other means of artistic expression,
whether the idiom used be music, painting, sculpture, or the written
or spoken word. In each case, the creative impulse comes first and is
essential; but the expression of this impulse is consciously controlled
and measured, eliminating any chance solution. A work of art
cannot be, I think, the result of a haphazard solution. The
development of the creative impulse is carried out by means of rhythms
which will produce what the artist knows to be the desired result.
In any art, the artist learns how to stress a sound, a word, a color, a line,
a shape, a volume, by means of contrast, comparison, repetition,
tension, and relaxation, slowing down speed for suspense, racing speed
for climax–and this, whether he is dealing with Mark Antony's funeral
oration in *Julius Caesar,* with the construction of Dostoyevsky's *The Idiot,*
with the counterpoint in a Bach fugue, with a Debussy sound picture,
a Picasso or Braque Cubist canvas, a Matisse color juxtaposition, a
Mondrian, or a Moore sculpture. In a Beethoven symphony, for instance,
the parts are linked to each other, from the statement of the theme
to the conclusion. In a garden, the theme stated may be the dominant

place given to a certain plant, or it may be the use of cylindrical flower boxes, repeated at various time intervals. If I wish to stress the vertical of a colonnade in a garden, it must be contrasted with the horizontal of a mosaic stone path at intervals in which I may plant low-growing volumes, such as a series of *Philodendron,* all different but all closely linked by their family characteristics.

The great difference, of course, between the two-dimensional painter and the three-dimensional landscape architect is that the plant–the raw material–is not static. It has its own cycle of bud, flower, seed, and withering; and then again, a gust of wind, a cloud, a shower, or a storm will alter its color and its very structure. The painting on the drawing board is not the garden itself, any more than a photograph of a Calder mobile can give you any real idea of the emotion aroused by a mobile in the open air. It is this particular aesthetic quality, which if the garden is properly planned, will produce in the spectator a constant state of exaltation and surprise. In the creation of these effects, the artist must use every means at his command. In addition to playing off a hot color against a cold color for contrast, as I did with a flower and mosaic garden in the 4th Centennial Gardens, or superimposing a hot color on a still hotter one for harmony, one must know which volume to use, given an equal coloring. Thus when planting a yellow-flowering tree one has the choice of the pendant flower cluster of the *Lophanthera lactescens,* or the erect pyramid of the *Caesalpinia peltophoroides*–the effect in space will be entirely different.

Every discovery of our modern age can be turned to advantage by artists: microphotography has made man familiar with amoebic shapes, which provide a contrast with the angular shapes of a building; aerial photography shows the relation that exists between the contours of the earth and of these amoebic shapes, and inspires us to use analogical repetition on a different scale, which is a valuable element in a garden.

And although my most recent gardens have developed a more constructional geometry, if asymmetrical form, as compared with the freer-flowing forms of my earlier gardens, there is nothing standardized here; the recreation island I designed for the heart-shaped lagoon has geometrical palm groves flanking a baroque building, but as the foliage beds spread out toward the lake, they will gradually break out into the freer forms of the island's topography, whose forms are analogous with those of the mountains in the distance.

How valuable these free forms have proved in the landscape garden I would like to show you now. When confronting the problem of foreshortening the landscape, bringing it into the garden, such as in the Odette Monteiro Garden, in Correias near Petrópolis in Rio de Janeiro state, where the house itself is in pseudo-colonial Portuguese Style,[19] the integration of the landscape with the garden is brought about by groups of boulders with plant groups that repeat the rock vegetation of the region, while the boulders echo the sheer granite of the mountain. The forest at its foot is brought closer to the garden by the strategic value given to the picturesque tree in the middle distance, while the kidney- or amoeba-shaped bed on the slope of the hill echoes the shape of the lake at the heart of the garden, mirroring the landscape for those who sit on the terrace outside the house. A further foreshortening is achieved by means of the stepping-stones which cross the lake, spreading themselves further and further apart as they march into the grass on the far side, toward the mountains. The feathery plumes of the *Cortaderia argentea* (pampas grass) and the flame pokers of the *Kniphofia* (torch lily) on the nearby hillside are pointers to the picturesque tree in the middle distance. The garden is a series of small groups linked together by such aesthetic intentions as I have described, producing an overall landscape intention, for which the windows of the house provide a frame; and fortunately, since the house is situated at the far end of the property from the mountain view, it has been possible to study the landscape architecture as a separate problem.[20]

A case in which the architecture, though not contemporary, must be taken into account, is that of the 18th-century farmhouse above Petrópolis, the Fazenda da Samambaia. Here the excellent proportions of the building and the Chinese effect of the up-pointed corners of the curved tile roof demand that texture and delicacy shall be the dominating features of this landscape. The large lake, mirroring small leaf and flower groups that slope from the house down to a lower path level; the ancient-style lamppost; and the rocks which merge in with the flower groups, create a romantic, picturesque effect, such as is found in Japanese and Chinese gardens. The free forms here are not sharply outlined as they would be in an abstract-painting garden, since the intention here is to create a mellow atmosphere of a landscaped garden of the past.

The problem of texture in ground cover, as William Kent explained and Glaziou exemplified in Passeio Público, is essentially a landscape problem, but it is one that has great interest for the abstract painter. In the Gavea Garden laid out 10 years ago for Mr. Almeida Braga, the painted lawns in abstract free-flowing forms vary in color: the *Stenotaphrum americanum Schrank* and the *Stenotaphrum americanum Schrank var. variegata* are sharply defined: one is green, and the other a bright lemon yellow. While the constructional note is provided by the semicircular blue-glaze tile bench in the traditional 19th-century pattern, forming the link between two groups of *Aloe attenuata,* used for their well-defined structural characteristics. The garden is not a foreshortening of the landscape; but the forest that clothes the hill is repeated by lower-growing trees and flowering or colored-foliage bushes, which, in their turn, are the link between the painted lawns and the forests, while waterfalls are called to mind by the little stream which flows between the garden and the hillside. Sculptural marginal plants, such as the *Cyperus papyrus* (paper reed) and *Pontederia cordata,* fuse with the boundary bushes and flowering trees.

The new garden I made for Carlos Somlo could not take the architecture into account either, since the house is a Tyrol châlet carried out with Brazilian building materials. The garden already contained some fine specimens of conifers that grow well at an altitude of 300 feet (900 meters) above sea level, in this gently sloping Cuiaba Valley looking toward distant blue mountains. A monotonous lawn surrounded the conifers in a slope with a slight depression in it. The conifers were too fine to uproot nor did I wish to plant any large tree volumes, which would spoil the open view toward the mountains and toward some beautiful trees with golden foliage in the middle distance. The fact that the conifers were to be the largest volumes pointed to the obvious solution of the use of fine-textured plants. Round the base of one of these trees there is a foliage bed planted with pink and green *Telantera amena,* which has a fabric-tapestry consistency, in free forms sharply divided from the metallic red of small-leaved *Iresine herbstii* (bloodleaf), and from the carmine of *Salvia splendens* (scarlet sage). The monotony of the lawn is now broken up by the use of white, lemon-yellow striped with cream, and green grasses (*Stenotaphrum americanum Schrank* and *Chlorophytum comosum,* or spider plants) in well-defined forms, echoing the contours of the slope as it falls toward the depression, which has been deepened to hold a small pool. Here, rounded stones echo the rhythm of the rounded cushions of red foliage, and a note of contrast has been created by the sharply vertical *Eleocharis fistulosa,* a reed never before used in a garden. This reed is relatively low-growing, and the largest volume contrasting with the marginal plants are the *Philodendron speciosum* and *Pundulatum* groups on a small rise in front of the pool.

Thus a rich and varied play of texture and color can be viewed from a semicircular granite bench formed by slabs with interstices filled with pebbles, a texture repeated in the flooring beneath the bench. To the left, protecting the bench, is a bush with many-fingered leaves and milk-white bunches of flowers, the *Tetrapanax papyrifer* (rice-paper plant) from Australia; while by analogy, to the right of the bench, but near to the pool, a group of Japanese *Fatsia japonica* (paper plant) with smaller leaves but with the same structure, has been planted. Behind the bench, the protective arms of the *Ficus roxburghii,* with its strange figs growing at ground level, act as a screen.

In the case of the prize-winning house at Bom Clima by Henrique Mindlin, also situated on a slope, the flowing forms were chosen in contrast to the angular fan of the architecture.[21] The garden was relatively small. A small lawn spreading from a free area under the pilotis was left without any large volume to give the impression of space, while to the left, on the slope, a painted foliage bed of low volumes contrasts the metallic texture of the *Iresine herbstii,* with the velvet pearl gray of the *Helichrysum plicatum.* Lower down the slope, a sculptural effect is provided by a mass of *Musa rosacea,* a banana plant with a particularly beautiful pink flower. The brilliant colors of a glass mosaic mural on an angular, freestanding wall-screen, under the pilotis, appear to create an extension of the garden right into the house area itself.

A complete integration of house and garden was attempted in the Walter Moreira Salles estate in Gavea, already mentioned. The house is built around a patio, the flooring of which is pinkish-red and white stone mosaic and beaten red brick, and in which the sculptural element is provided by *Dracaena marginata* (dragon plant) and by *Beaucarnea* (ponytail palm), on which grow various varieties of the *Cattleya* orchid. The link between all architectural and garden sections is made by means of the same stone mosaic, or *Pedra Portuguesa* as we call it, used for paths, continued beyond the three sides of the house round the patio, leading on one side in dramatic curves to the water lily pool backed by the sinuous 20-meter wall, faced with a glazed-tile mural in a water carrier design, and on the other side, in a free but more angular form, leading to the turquoise-lined swimming pool. The water carrier mural, topped by a row of plants, faces the wall, ensuring privacy from the servants' quarters (the house belongs to an ex-ambassador and president of a bank), while it also reflects the pool, into which jets pour water from the glazed tiles out of nine thin pipes. Aquatic plants grow in a concrete box hidden under the surface of the pool, and form small sculptural designs against the semirealistic forms of the panel. The dining room window frames this curving view, thus once more uniting the house with the garden. In another wing, a balustraded corridor looks down on a sharply angular abstract foliage parterre of broderie, which I have already shown you, and in which texture is subordinated to brilliant color, with the contrasting volume being provided by the Venetian-red bush of an *Acalypha wilkesiana,* surrounding the parterre.

In a São Paulo garden where neither the house nor the view could be used, I had to concentrate in a relatively small space sufficient interest to focus the entire attention of the spectator.[22] This was achieved by means of starting, in a group of trees, an undulating freestanding wall, faced with glass mosaic in geometrical designs with large areas of grays, blues, and reds, stressing verticals and horizontals.

The colors were then completed by planting beneath it low-growing foliage with contrasting color: a gray plant against a red section of wall, a red plant against a blue. In addition, the verticals of the panel were completed by the verticals of the slender tree trunks, while the two-dimensional character of the panel was accentuated by the sculptural plants growing against the cooler patches of color.

If I have not mentioned in detail the 4th Centennial Gardens, the Ibirapuera Park in São Paulo, it is because they demand a much more detailed explanation than is possible here. As I have said, a two-dimensional painting cannot give a full idea of a three-dimensional group of gardens covering 4 million square feet (about 400,000 square meters), and in which such elements as cylindrical flower boxes rise from the bottom to the surface of a mosaic-faced pool; and in which in another garden, water is used as sculpture, along a fountain path where vertical, illuminated jets rise from chessboard patterns of plants and foliage; or again in which, a raised path, cantilevered like a switchback railway over a plant puzzle of brilliantly colored flowers and foliage, gives man a spatial experience which varies as he views the garden and the sculpture in it from different heights and angles.

In another opportunity, I have planned to describe these gardens which, had they been carried out, would have been the summing-up of the experiences of 20 years. Together with these, I hoped to describe other gardens, such as those of the Ministry of Education and Health from 1936 to 1938, the roof garden of the Reseguros Insurance Building, and others which have their place in the development of my work.

But the most important point, and I stress it once again, is the human contact with ordered nature that must never be lost sight of when planning a garden. I have tried, even where the garden is almost a park, such as that of the Odette Monteiro Garden, the Fazenda Marambaia, to relate all the component parts to one to another in such a manner as not to lose sight of the man who walks its paths, crosses its lake by the stepping-stones, or stands beside its trees. Thus, he will not be dwarfed by the size of the garden nor lose his feeling of a right to his position in space. This is what he had, as he strolled along the paths at Stowe in the 18th century, and this is what he now needs, whatever the type of garden he can still walk in, in this overcrowded 20th-century world.

1   Originally, "landscape gardener" but in the hand-annotated version of this lecture, Roberto Burle Marx had crossed out "gardener" and replaced it with "architect." Haruyoshi Ono told me that this was a deliberate vocabulary shift, as Burle Marx was sensitive to not being regarded as a landscape architect by many of his peers.
2   The Burton Tremaine Residence in Santa Barbara, California, was designed by Oscar Niemeyer, with the garden by Roberto Burle Marx in 1948. Although unbuilt, the plan is one of the most iconic of Burle Marx's drawings.
3   See Philip L. Goodwin, *Brazil Builds: Architecture New and Old, 1652–1942* (New York: Museum of Modern Art, 1943).
4   Le Corbusier first visited Brazil in 1929.
5   Unverified quotation.
6   Originally, "landscaper" but changed to "landscape architect" by Burle Marx in the hand-annotated version.
7   A bract is a modified leaf or scale at the base of a flower, and the bracts of *Heliconia* are sometimes mistaken for the flowers. In fact, the *Heliconia* bracts obscure the small flowers. *Heliconia* are sometimes called "parrot flowers" because of the beak shape and colors of the bracts.
8   Originally, "landscaper."
9   Originally, "landscaped."
10 The imperial palm was not actually planted until 1809. See Roseli D'Elboux, "A Promenade in the Tropics: The Imperial Palms between Rio de Janeiro and São Paulo," *Studies in the History of Gardens and Designed Landscape* 33, no. 3 (2013):148–56.
11 Originally, "landscaper."
12 Pernambuco is a state in northeast Brazil.
13 Describing Lúcio Costa as "the true father of contemporary Brazilian architecture" was perhaps intended as a slight on Oscar Niemeyer, who is more often than not assumed to hold this position, and would have held this position at the time of the lecture.
14 Candido Portinari (1903–1962) was one of the most important 20th-century Brazilian painters, and Burle Marx's instructor at the Escola de Belas Artes in Rio de Janeiro. Leo Putz (1869–1940) was also a painter and professor at the Escola de Belas Artes. He moved to Brazil in 1929 at Lúcio Costa's invitation.
15 Gregori Warchavchik (1896–1972) was a Ukrainian-Brazilian architect, and one of the pioneers of Brazilian modern architecture.
16 The roof garden of Alfredo Schwartz House, Rio de Janeiro, 1932.
17 André Le Nôtre (1613–1700) is best known for designing the landscape at the Château de Versailles for Louis XIV.
18 The Ministry of Education and Health Building in Rio de Janeiro was constructed in 1935 with blue and white glazed tile murals.
19 The house was designed by Wladimir Alves de Souza.
20 Originally, "landscaping."
21 Bom Clima was built in 1949 and was awarded the prize of the first Biennial of Architecture in São Paulo in 1951.
22 Dating from 1956, originally the garden of the Francisco Pignatari Residence and now known as the Burle Marx Park.

The Problem
of Garden Lighting

Undated English translation, but from the reference
to the Civic Center of Curitiba we can assume it dates
from the mid-1960s.

With the advent of electricity and its use for the production of artificial light, new possibilities of expression arose to give an equally new dimension and, consequently, a novel and integral utilization to the garden.[1] To date, the use of electricity in the garden has been conceived in a static manner, by fixed points of luminous irradiation, with the sole purpose of giving a feeling of safety to the persons who walk by parks or green areas, without great imagination in its customary use.

Let us have a look at nature during the day: we will see infinite variations produced by the sunlight in its constant movement. Atmospheric conditions change one color in a surface into a thousand shades, creating transparencies in the foliage or emphasizing the splendor of blossoming. Light creates variable centers of interest by projecting the shadow of the clouds brought by the wind, and drawing focus to now one and now another detail of the landscape we are contemplating. The Impressionists, in investigating the phenomenon of the duration of the luminous impression on the retina, and in re-creating the atmosphere in color, knew how to bring forth in marvelous paintings the nuances produced by the sunlight in different seasons, landscapes, or objects, showing their beauty in their changing hues,[2] as for instance, in the series of the Rouen Cathedral by Claude Monet.[3]

Certainly, we cannot affirm that we are always willing to intensely distinguish these variations. We all know that, according to our internal disposition, we are happy or sad, depending on the circumstances which influence our conscious and unconscious mind. The ability to perceive the beauty of things varies at the same pace with which we apprehend a certain situation.[4]

But man has always tried—by re-creating them—to grasp and enhance the conditions wrought by natural phenomena which elude his will, so that he can command them with the specific purpose of reaping their advantages. One phenomena which has captivated his imagination is light: it was identified with the divine, with everything which is good, and as a symbol of intelligence and regeneration. In religions, temples have been built to enhance the greatness and the mystery of the deity: the light, shining in the twilight of rooms where only the initiated were accepted, indicated the presence of the divine. In Catholic churches, the small lamp in the sanctuary reminds the faithful of the presence

of God in the tabernacle. A candle next to the dying lights up the
passage through the kingdom of shadows. In processions, lit candles
are the means of showing the path of those who have faith to
a brighter world. In Afro-Brazilian rituals, it is enough to remember
the Iemanjá celebration, in which the candles enter into a dialogue
with the supernatural and mark the outline of beaches with a light that
comes from holes dug in the sand, illuminating figures from below
upwards.[5]

Brightness and darkness: contrasts of good and evil, angel and devil
–mystical images for all peoples.

In Greek mythology, man wanted to know the secret of the
production of light. Prometheus stole fire and was condemned: this fire
was needed for the preservation of the species and should be kept
burning.[6] First, the need for fire; subsequently, the rite and the creation
of the Vestal Virgins, the guardians who cultivated the sacred fire.[7]
The constructors of the Gothic cathedrals fully understood the quality
of light to induce the mind to focus on the divine, by creating an
atmosphere of suggestive dimness and a structure made out of courage
and audacity, directing all glances heavenward. The light filters through
the stained glass windows, falling in the fissures of the pilasters,
wisely oriented to emphasize the splendor of the altar, and intended
to raise the spirits, like the structure of ships, in the extreme purity of
its constructive system.

The light at night, in the streets and alleys of old cities, was provided
by vacillating torches, the light flickering with the wind, creating shadows
bodied in the imagination as ghosts and which spread terror in
the Middle Ages. In homes, the light of the candle, also flickering, made
furniture glow, or faces shine around a table. Candlelight is the image
of life, the creative consuming work, or the sacrifice it represents: the
anguish of the petitioner who lights a candle before a statue of a saint
in church.

The ritual of the daily lighting and putting out of candles, the slow
gestures of ladies holding candelabra, the splendor of the crystal.
A ritual which reaches its dramatic peak at the Tenebrae ceremony in
the Holy Week liturgy,[8] when the priest intoning the prayers puts out
one by one the candles of the triangular candelabrum, until complete

darkness falls: and afterwards he lights up all candles again, suggesting death and resurrection.

With the Counter-Reformation, the Church felt the need to follow the new ideals brought about by the Renaissance and the Baroque: therefore, the interiors of churches became brighter, the space was expanded with new construction techniques, and light suddenly penetrated the interior, reaching a maximum, for instance, in the Basilica of the Fourteen Holy Helpers, of the German Baroque.[9]

At the same time, with the Church no longer the most important patron of the arts, and with the increasing power of kings and queens, artists turned their imaginations toward exalting earthly rather than heavenly power. At the inauguration of Vaux-le-Vicomte,[10] at the end of the festivities thousands of lights were lit suddenly, showing the groups of sculptures, making them reflect in the canal or in the lakes: the garden became all brilliant with the fireworks, in a *féerie* of incomparable magnificence.[11]

These considerations as an introduction may induce one to think that we miss the old times,[12] and that this longing would lead us to repeat solutions–which in that period and with the possibilities of that moment proved to be valid but, if revived, would lose all their enchantment and would distort their original purpose.[13]

We went back in time to find out how men have illuminated nights with extraordinary imagination and scarce means, and we wanted to take advantage of that lesson to extract the quality bequeathed to us by our forefathers: not to imitate, but to re-create, using new possibilities, such as those offered by electricity and lasers.

In the theater, the possibilities of lighting have been explored to the utmost: light is controlled, intensified, directed in accordance with the mood suggested by the play. Light effects are used to dramatically emphasize a particular state of mind in stage scenes devoid of objects, connecting research on color and reasons for the traditional utilization of certain colors for specific states of mind. White, for instance, is always linked to purity; black, to absence and death; purple, to pain; red and bright colors to the joy of living. This, plus studies on sound effects, is an avenue toward the search for an essential language that ignores circumstances.

These new possibilities may be used in the garden, as it is the place where we behave as actors, where we get acquainted with nature as an aesthetic phenomenon and a manifestation of life. Gardens are generally used during the day. At night they do not provide all the advantage they could.

In a theater, light follows the actors while they are moving. In a garden, it is the light that should move through the apparent stability of plant groups.

However, when we think on lighting for the garden landscape, we immediately think of the lamppost: small or big, the problem of lighting still lacks a solution. For example, huge lampposts were placed in the Flamengo Park in Rio de Janeiro,[14] breaking the scale of the park and the landscape of Guanabara Bay, without bringing any new idea in lighting and without any imagination or technical criteria in their indiscriminate placement, because reflectors still had to be used in the sports fields. In the several gas stations that are in the park, the type of lighting used would have been better suited for a highway.

Taking advantage of the possibilities of controlling the intensity of light, a spotlight could be used in a garden to illuminate a group of foliage, showing the nervures and transparencies of the leaves; a tree with an odd form; the texture of a trunk; thus creating varied centers of interest in the garden; or showing the blossoming of certain plants, as for instance, *Cereus jamacaru* (a very tall cactus) or *Nymphaea* (a genus of water lilies) in rhythmic movements, which have already been beautifully shown in the movies.

In San Antonio, Texas, I saw a section of a small river illuminated, where the supports for the spotlights were the trees themselves, clearly showing the path and the texture of the trunks which supported them.[15]

In the project for the Civic Center of Curitiba,[16] the lighting of the square will be indirect: there are three great lakes with water jets of 20–30 feet (6 to 10 meters) height, placed in sequences and illuminated intensely from below, using the water not only as a vivifying element but also as a dynamic sculpture, softly reflecting the light in the square and benefiting from the multiple possibilities of diffraction, reflection, and refraction when falling on the water column. In other areas of the square, the lateral facades of the palaces will be illuminated from below and while the trees are still juvenile, reflectors will be placed in their canopies and directed toward the points of interest: the pavement, made in patterns of Portuguese stone, the benches, and even the trees, as well as the colored surfaces. But there are still other possibilities for the garden, which have not been used yet: a combined use of light, color, and related sculptural elements in a dynamic manner, such as by placing sculptures in the garden, and grouping them so they can be included in the composition, giving each one a special surrounding by means of colored walls or greenish surfaces, which will enhance them during the day and could be highlighted at night from various angles. A combination of light, color, and sculptural elements could be used in a dynamic manner to reveal the points of interest, which would otherwise in daylight go unnoticed.[17]

The same could be said about certain plants of a distinct structure and sculptural form, as for instance *Ceiba erianthus* or the blossoming of *Heliconia.* Lit at night, the garden serves to verify the work of nature: continuously developing themes with rich variation and solutions.

But one must not think that all in a garden should be in the foreground and manifested. It is necessary to give to the person who is enjoying it the idea of what is near and what is distant: the idea that, in the garden, there are moments of greatest intensity and of calm and rest. Pierre Boulez said, about music paying homage to Anton Webern, "One of the most difficult truths to make evident is that music is not only an art of sounds, but that it is better defined by a counterpoint of sound and silence."[18] Likewise, in the garden, as in all other composition, art always uses contrasts and analogies in a work of synthesis and in search of its own language.

In accord with this thought, we pointed out in the beginning of our lecture how wisely the ancients knew to take advantage of their possibilities, and we realize that some uses of artificial light in the garden are delineated so that we may find the secret which gives us depth today, makes us improve spiritually, each gesture bringing us a reason for enchantment and reminding us that we are not automatons.

Art is not merely a triumph over technical difficulties, although this is one of its elements. "The technical point of view is not opposed to the spiritual point of view; one is a raw material while the other is the masterpiece. One does not live without the other," as Le Corbusier said.

So art is a reconciliation of life conflicts, indicating the ways man may find his true essence.

To sum up, we wish to say that **the garden is a vast field of experiences for the visual arts, by its deep links with the problems of architecture and urbanism,** besides being a place which provides for the development of man and of his creative powers, his heedfulness, and his desire to communicate with his fellow men and with nature.

Original text used for comparing the translation: Roberto Burle Marx, "Jardim e iluminação artificial," in *Arte e paisagem: conferências escolhidas,* ed. José Tabacow (São Paulo: Nobel, 2004), 77–84.

1   "…an equally new dimension and, consequently…" This is present in the Portuguese edition but is absent from the English translation.

2   Original:…*mostrando a sua beleza em matizes cambiantes…*

3   In the 1890s, Monet painted more than forty views of the facade of Rouen Cathedral in differing lights.

4   Original:…*varia, assim, com a rapidez com que apreendemos.*

5   Iemanjá is an Afro-Brazilian orisha (*orixá*), energy of nature, and deity often syncretized with Our Lady of the Seafaring (*Nossa Senhora dos Navegantes*); "A candle next to the dying…illuminate supernatural figures from below" is present in the Portuguese edition but absent from the English translation; Original: *Nos rituais afro-brasileiros, basta lembrar a festa de Iemanjá, em que as velas entram nesse diálogo com o sobrenatural e marcam o contorno das praias com uma luz que vem de buracos cavados na areia, a iluminar as figuras de baixo para cima.*

6   Prometheus is a Greek god, creator of humans, who stole fire from Mount Olympus against the will of Zeus, for the benefit of humankind.

7   Original: *Primeiro a necessidade; posteriormente, o rito e a insinuação das vestais, virgens guardiãs do fogo sagrado.*

8   A Christian ritual, performed for three
     days prior to Easter. Usually 15 candles
     are extinguished one by one while
     prayers and psalms are recited.
9   The *Basilika Vierzehnheiligen* near
     Bamberg, Germany.
10   Situated 30 miles (about 50 kilometers)
     southeast of Paris, Vaux-le-Vicomte
     was inaugurated on August 17, 1661.
     Candlelight evenings, with up to 2,000
     lighted candles, are still celebrated in
     the gardens during the summer
     months.
11   Original, *feérico,* in the Portuguese,
     meaning part of a fantasy world,
     a world of dreams. Burle Marx used
     the French word, *féerie,* in the
     English translation.
12   Original: *Essas considerações, como
     introdução, poderiam induzir
     a pensar…,* "To introduce with those
     thoughts/comments could induce
     to think…"
13   Original: *…e falseariam a sua
     finalidade,* "and would distort the
     intention/the purpose."
14   The Flamengo Park (1954–1964)
     landfill project was planned by a group
     of designers led by Maria Carlota
     de Macedo Soares, with Roberto Burle
     Marx as the landscape architect.
15   Original: *…vi um trecho de um
     pequeno rio iluminado, no qual
     o suporte das luminárias eram as
     próprias árvores, mostrando bem
     tanto o caminho quanto…*
16   Dating from 1966, Jose Tabacow
     worked with Burle Marx on the project.
     The architectural team included Olavo
     Redig de Campos and David Azambuja.
17   Original: *Mostrando pontos de
     interesse que, às vezes, à plena luz,
     passam despercebidos…*
18   Pierre Boulez (1925–2016) was a
     French conductor, composer, and
     writer.

Landscapes of Brazil

Undated lecture.

The enormous area of Brazil and the diversity of its soil, geological conditions, its latitudinal position and the consequent variations in climate, contribute toward the existence of one of the richest and most varied flora in the world. It may be subdivided into six principal types:

The forests, including the enormous surface area of the Amazon rainforest, which constitutes about 40 percent of the territory of Brazil and one of the greatest forest masses in the world; the tropical forest on the Atlantic coast and in the interior; and the sub-tropical forest, which is also called the Pine Zone, or the region of the Araucaria.

The Caatinga, which contains a multitude of vegetable forms of xerophytic habit and an abundance of plants that are deciduous in hot and dry seasons.[1]

The Cerrado, which covers the greater part of the high plain of Brazil, and separates one half of the Amazon forest from the tropical forest of the interior.[2]

The Campos, which can be further sub-divided into (i) the southern plateau and the south part of Mato Grosso, which are principally grasslands; (ii) the higher plains, which exist between 3,000 and 40,000 feet (about 1,000 and 12,000 meters) above sea level, and which have an abundance of Velloziaceae and Melastomataceae (of genera *Lavoisiera, Chaetostoma,* etc.); whose vegetation changes its aspect according to whether it is wet or dry.[3]

The Pantanal Complex,[4] whose vegetation is rich in aquatic species and is confined to the southern part of the state of Mato Grosso.

And, finally, the coastal areas, with mangroves, the vegetation of the beaches, and other sandy regions.

The classification of these zones was originally that of Carl Friedrich Philipp von Martius, who recognized their principal features and gave them names with a delightfully mythological flavor, such as Oreades, for the coastal region, Hamadryades for the Caatinga, Napeaea for the sub-tropical region of the Araucaria and so on. Later, Adolf Engler, in his phytogeographical picture of the world, was to follow approximately this classification, though with some modification. An important contribution was made by Professor Alberto do Sampaio of the Museu Nacional in Rio de Janeiro. He adapted the classifications of Martius and created a new specific formulation, including a new zone, that of the coconuts, which contained palm trees like the buriti, the babaçu, and the carnaúba. Later studies were to show that this was a transitional area between the flora of the Amazon and other regions.[5]

I should like, very briefly, to mention some characteristics of the different zones of vegetation. The forests, for instance, are notable for the presence of huge trees, which are adapted particularly to great heat and enormous rainfall;[6] in some cases, particularly in the forest of the *Araucaria* a genus of (evergreen coniferous trees), they have a character relatively more homogenous than the others, owing to the existence of narrower ecological relationships with the animal world and to other factors, such as altitude, the distance of the sea, and the nature of the soil.

The Caatinga is defined by its marked periodicity; there are very definite periods of dormancy. The green disappears—except for that of the Cactaceas (a family of succulents) and some evergreen trees such as the *Ziziphus joazeiro*—and the whole countryside, the soil and the leafless vegetation, becomes a yellowish brown, only to be transformed after rain into a veritable garden by the rapid growth of laminated leaves and exuberant flowering.

The Cerrado has a very different surface character, owing to the presence of small trees with twisted trunks and thick bark and broad leaves. They grow principally on soils usually deep and permeable, but whose mineral wealth is constantly impoverished by having its more movable elements, such as potassium and phosphorous, washed away by underground streams. Certain animals are also frequent and indigenous to this kind of country, among them the wolf, the emu, and the rattlesnake. Below the trees there is a residue of leaves and grasses which, drying quickly, serve as the starting point for the enormous forest fires which sweep across central Brazil and which made such an impression on the biologist Eugen Warming.[7]

The Campos are of a very diverse nature, and notable principally for the low vegetation which dominates and above all for the seasonal flowering, particularly in the southern plateau, which produces wave after wave of solid color, covering enormous areas.

The Pantanal region of swamps and marshes grows over the remains of an ancient inland sea and is entirely governed by the existence of this marine era.[8] The coastal vegetation is conditioned by the proximity of the sea, with its influence on wind, salinity, and the quality of the light.[9]

The Brazilian flora is of such splendor, covering as it does a country as huge and varied as Brazil, that its richness has been mentioned right from the beginning. In the very first document written by a man from Europe, the letter from Pero Vaz de Caminha to the King of Portugal,[10] he writes, in addition to the indigenous inhabitants and the native birds, of its trees and its algae. The French, who tried very hard to establish their position on Brazilian soil, left documents about its natural history, in particular those of André Thevet and Jean de Léry.

The first studies of the flora of a scientific nature were those made by the naturalists brought to Brazil by Prince Mauritius of Orange, Georg Marcgrave, and Willem Piso. On the Portuguese side, the highest point was the voyage of discovery undertaken by Alexandre Rodrigues Ferreira (from the state of Bahia) who, in the course of many years, traveled through territory now contained by the states of Pará, Amazonas, and Mato Grosso, collecting and drawing plants, animals, minerals, and ethnographical specimens; and this immense and valuable document has, sadly, still never been published. More fortunate was the friar José Mariano da Conceição Velloso, who over many years made voyages of discovery into the interior of the region of what today is the state of Rio de Janeiro, which resulted in elaborate manuscripts and drawings of the *Flora Fluminensis.* Although published after his death, resulting in a series of mistakes and misunderstandings, it remains in its own right an iconographical work of considerable rarity.[11]

The 19th century was the great period of Brazilian botany. Martius, supported by the Empress Leopoldina, started to work on the monumental *Flora Brasiliensis,* which received the support of the reigning houses of Brazil, Austria, and Bavaria. For 65 years, 66 botanists and dozens of collectors gathered material, on which was founded a most complete collection of tropical flora. The 19th century was, particularly, the century of great travels and remarkable travelers. Augustin Saint-Hilaire traveled through the southern provinces, as well as Minas Gerais and Espírito Santo. Carl Axel Magnus Lindman crossed the state of Rio Grande do Sul. Friedrich Sellow made important collections in southern Brazil and ended by dying tragically in the basin of the Rio Doce. Charles Gaudichaud-Beaupré explored the coastal regions and George Gardner ventured into the Serra dos Orgãos, crossing the Northeast diagonally. Prince Maximilian of Wied-Neuwied examined Espírito Santo and the southern part of Bahia.

In that century and at the beginning of the 20th century, in addition to illustrious foreigners, there were several important Brazilian botanists. Brother Leandro do Sacramento, a German friar, doctor, and professor of botany, published numerous works and directed the Scientific Commission of the Province of Ceara. Ladislau de Souza Mello Netto, director of the Museu Nacional, had republished, for their archives,[12] the text of the *Flora Fluminensis* by Velloso. At the turn of the 19th to the 20th century, two remarkable scientists, João Barbosa Rodrigues of the Rio de Janeiro Botanical Gardens and João Baptista de Lacerda of the Museu Nacional, maintained a lively dispute over the botanical origin of curare, and drew international attention to Brazilian science by the vigor of their arguments.[13]

The first half of the 20th century is remarkable for the presence of a group of botanists of German origin. Frederico Carlos Hoehne served as director of *Flora Brasilica,* an experiment to update the *Flora* by Martius. João Kuhlmann, a botanist to the Rondon Commission and director of the Rio Botanical Gardens, studied the nomenclature of an enormous number of Brazilian forest trees. Adolpho Ducke, the botanist of the Amazonas, dedicated the major part of his life to discovering the Amazonian flora. Alexander Brade, orchidologist and lepidopterist, although retired, continued to work regularly and with enthusiasm on his monographs. Henrique Lahmeyer de Mello Barreto, director of the old Botanical Garden at Belo Horizonte and, later of the Zoological Garden of Rio de Janeiro, became famous for his studies of the flora of Minais Gerais, publishing a comprehensive description of the phytogeographical divisions of this region. Finally, Alberto José Sampaio, of the Museu Nacional, deserves special mention for his general erudition, for his knowledge of botany in almost every field, and above all, for his superb capacity as a teacher.[14] He promoted the first meeting of the Conservation of Nature and left a large body of scientific work, in particular *Phytogeographical of Brazil* and *Flora of the Rio Cuminá.*[15]

The cultivation of native plants and the introduction of foreign ones went hand in hand after the initiation of these activities by the creation of the Jardim da Aclimação (Garden of Acclimatization) by Dom João VI which was later followed by the establishment of the the Botanical Gardens. This garden also introduced the imperial palm (Palma Mater, the "Mother of Palms"), whose progeny form one of the most important elements in our urban landscape, offering a link between architecture, man, and nature.

The Second Empire introduced a new period with Auguste Marie François Glaziou, whose presence we are still able to feel through the works he has left us, combining plants imported from the great European nursery companies, such as Vilmorin and Andrieux, with native Brazilian plants. Glaziou, a botanist and landscape gardener, made collections in central Brazil and the riverside areas and created the most beautiful parks in Rio de Janeiro–the Quinta da Boa Vista and Campo de Santana–as well as other less important works. The Avenue of Sapucaias at Quinta da Boa Vista, both by its intrinsic beauty and by its capacity for persistence, has received the admiration of successive generations. Glaziou can be considered, without exaggeration, the author of the most important piece of landscape architecture in our country.[16]

Brazilian floriculture has other landmarks, such as the contributions of Binot Paulmier de Gonneville, also a constructor of gardens; of Schlick of the Casa Flora, who popularized a great many ornamental plants imported by him; and the Chácara Hortolândia, a business which specialized in the growing of fruit trees and the cultivation of palms. Very important also was the action of the gardener Adolph Lietze, who produced a collection of caladiums for hybridization, the results of which are distributed and cultivated throughout the world. His memory is preserved by the beautiful plant *Calathea lietzei.*

The flowering of horticulture came as a consequence of the Victorian epoch, in which the steamship made possible both the botanical exploration of all the continents, and the rapid transport of the collected plants to the hothouses of England. Our most recent phase is dominated by the Germans, who have tried to improve on the results of the Victorian age in a competition that has come too late.[17] As a result of their labors, we have roses of the finest quality introduced by João Dierberger, together with many European ornamental shrubs (such as *Pyracantha*). All of the German gardeners who have made gardens in Brazil have one thing constant in their work, a kind of nostalgia for the European environment. Their gardens are classical and divorced from the realities of Brazil. One among them, Germano Zimber, of São Paulo, deserves to be mentioned for having cultivated a series of *Tibouchinas,* which are today very frequent in that landscape, giving to it sudden brushstrokes of beauty. Rinaldi, also of São Paulo, is distinguished for his cultivation of orchids, as is Rolf Altenburg, of Rio de Janeiro.

I personally have introduced many exotic ornamental plants, especially groups of *Philodendron, Maranta, Anthurium,* aquatic plants, and ornamental trees. This has not been to neglect the local flora. In this field I have been very much preoccupied with preserving an authentic reservoir of our plant life, today more than ever threatened by destruction on a massive scale–thoughtless, swift, and irretrievable– which continues, side by side, with our demographical explosion and with the perfection of the machines which exploit our forests and which exterminate whatever gets in their way.[18]

Original text used for comparing the translation: Roberto Burle Marx, "Horticultura no Brasil," in *Arte e paisagem: conferências escolhidas,* ed. José Tabacow (São Paulo: Nobel, 2004), 35–39.

1   Xerophytes are plants that require very little water to survive.
2   Original: *com disjunçõe no meio da floresta amazõnica.*
3   Original: *nos períodos de cheia ou de seca.*
4   Original: *O complex do Pantanal,* "The complex of Pantanal" / the several areas that compose the Pantanal.
5   Original: *extra-amazônica.*
6   Original: *marcadsa por condições especiais de pluviosidade e de insolação.*
7   Eugenius (Eugen) Warming (1841–1924) was a Danish botanist and a founding figure of ecology as a scientific discipline. Warming's field research on the processes of the Brazilian Cerrado (1863–1866) influenced his early publications on plant ecology.
8   Original: *período de inundação.*
9   Original: *com suas influências de vento, salsugem e luminosidade.*
10   Original: *a carta de Pero Vaz de Caminha,* "the letter from Pero Vaz de Caminha" [to the King of Portugal, Manual I, written in April 1500].
11   José Mariano de Conceição Vellozo (1742–1811) was a Brazilian botanist, whose most notable publication was *Flora Fluminensis.*
12   Original:*...faz publicar, nos arquivos daquela instituição.*
13   Original: *contribuição científica.*
14   Original: *capacidade didática.*
15   Alberto José Sampaio (1881–1946) was a Brazilian botanist. *Flora Do Rio Cuminá* was published in 1932 or 1933, and *Phytogeographia do Brasil* in 1934.
16   Originally, "landscaping."
17   Original: *numa competição tardia.*
18   Original: *da cobertura vegetal da terra.*

Landscape Projects for Large Areas

This lecture was delivered at Iowa State University in October 1962. Its title derives from a Portuguese-language edition of the talk published as, "Projetos de Paisagismo de Grandes Áreas," in *Arte e Paisagem: Conferências Escolhidas,* ed. José Tabacow (São Paulo: Nobel, 2004), 41–49. The Portuguese version, also dating from 1962, is substantially different, although with a similar basis, and the English lecture is reproduced here with minor edits.

At the present time, I am particularly concerned with the large
public park projects which are in the course of development in three
countries in South America, and are the results of the work with
my partners, John Stoddart, Fernando Tabora, and Julio Pessolari.
Because of their nature and size, they make new demands on
the landscape architect but also offer new opportunities: they suggest
an enormous range of solutions and encourage experimentation
and the expression of fresh ideas. In Venezuela, the Parque del Este
(150 acres of public park) is under construction a few miles from the
center of Caracas. In Brasília we have projected a zoo-botanical garden
(which is what its name suggests, a combination of a zoological
and a botanical garden, in addition to which it will serve as a city park).
In Rio de Janeiro there is the Flamengo Beach development, the
design of a 3-mile strip of waterfront reclaimed from Guanabara Bay;
it is nothing short of a miracle that the city administration has seen
fit to preserve it as a public park. In Santiago, Chile, the United Nations
Park (or Parque de Las Americas) has reached the preliminary
design stage. And finally, we are working on the layout of the Botanical
Garden of São Paulo, a project which unites the three functions of
an ecological botanical garden: a forest reservation for the protection
and preservation of fauna and flora, and a recreation park for the
residents of this booming and busy metropolis.

In the planning of these projects we have no doubt drawn upon
my experience of nearly 30 years of working with gardens. And so
it would not be out of place to comment upon some of my early works
at the outset of my career, such as the public gardens in the state
of Pernambuco, in the northeast of Brazil. In one of those gardens, the
gardens of Praça Euclídes da Cunha, I sought to make an ecological
garden featuring the plants of the Caatinga region and an aquatic garden
using in one section of exotic plants of Central and South America
and elsewhere plants from the Amazon basin. The Caatinga, I should
explain, is a region in the Northeast characterized by spiny plants,
which thrive under particularly dry and arid conditions. For many months
the plants appear as dead sticks, lifeless skeletons, and suddenly
after a period of heavy rains–almost overnight, the green leaves appear
as convincing and long-awaited evidence of life. By reproducing the

soil conditions of the Caatinga I was able to transplant associated species characteristic of this environment and use them in a public garden in Recife, a city in the Northeast once dominated by the Dutch, and which incidentally was the scene of the first painting of tropical plants by Frans Post and Albert Eckhout,[1] and botanical studies by Georg Marcgrave in the 17th and 18th centuries.[2]

The interpretation for the aquatic gardens came from a picture I saw of the large tanks of water plants at Kew Gardens, outside London. As a matter of fact, my biggest problem in this project was not a horticultural one at all: it involved the preservation or elimination of a hideous cement-rendered monument dedicated to the heroes of that state, or something or other. As expected, there was a strong anti-destructionist reaction from the local people and my only defense was that the monument, on account of its incongruity and monstrous ugliness, was not up to the standard of the heroes to which it was dedicated. Oddly enough, in visiting Kew many years later, I was surprised to see how different the actual aquatic gardens were from what I had constructed in my imagination.

To diverge for a moment, I would like to say a few words about the problem of monuments. In most Latin American cities there is an unfortunate predisposition toward hero-worship and the glorification of the dead, which results in the erection of a great many monuments. Irrespective of worthiness of the person being commemorated, they are invariably conceived on the lowest imaginable artistic level. Many are crude and vulgar, grotesque caricatures of the figures which they are meant to represent. In Rio, for example, there is such a preponderance of busts—I mean head-and-shoulder figures on short columns—that I once reached the point of imagining a public square occupied only by statues, in which the introduction of a single tree would be a subject for wild celebration.

To return to what I was saying about the lessons of my early works, much of what I have learned about public parks and in particular the construction of ecological gardens was acquired during the period I was working with my botanist friend Henrique Lahmeyer de Mello Barreto on the park of Araxá in the state of Minas Gerais, in the early 1940s. Associating with this botanist has been for me a wonderfully instructive experience. With him I visited and analyzed, one by one, the different plant associations of the hills of Minas Gerais. Together we identified the flora of different geological formations—sandstone, canga (conglomerate of iron), limestone, granite gneiss, and others—each of which supported a different and distinguishable plant community. Many years previously I had my first ecological lesson in Berlin when I saw the geographical sections created by Adolf Engler.

So much for background. I think this will give you some idea of my personal development, and of the past experiences which now influence my work on the large-scale public parks I am currently developing. In approaching the problem of a public recreation area, I believe the initial decision is one of meaning and intention. It is necessary to identify and isolate the most important considerations and, having established the priorities, to develop the design with them in mind. For example, in the case of the botanical garden, the design may be organized on the basis of a systematic grouping of plants by families or botanical divisions, or on the basis of an ecological grouping of species which tend to associate in particular habitats, or on the basis of a more or less eclectic principle which incorporates the best of both methods. Some groups based upon family characteristics (for example, the collections of Araceae, Bromeliaceae, Orchidaceae, Palmaceae, Marantaceae) offer great scope for aesthetic arrangement, so much so that they are almost an indispensable element of any botanical garden. Other plants are more effectively displayed in ecological sequences and arrangements, as I have previously suggested. The point I am making is that the landscape architect must be thoroughly familiar with the nature of a given problem, and seek a solution which combines both the functional and aesthetic requirements. To achieve this objective, he cannot merely reproduce nature or copy her habits; neither can he indulge in fancy completely divorced from reality. He is required to construct an artifice, something which is unquestionably the product of the inventive and creative mind of man (and to that extent is unnatural or rather, *more* than natural or perhaps supernatural), something which synthesizes purpose, meaning, use, and need with the artistic aspirations of the designer.

The introduction of animals into a park imposes other disciplines upon the design. The movement of animals and people must be separated without being entirely divorced from each other: the animals must be securely enclosed, and the public must be able to observe them without undue obstruction or interference. And these apparently conflicting requirements must be solved through the creation of a landscape that unites and exemplifies both functions. In the design for the Zoo-Botanical Garden of Brasília, I am endeavoring to display the animals against appropriate backgrounds, incorporating plant material characteristic of certain ecological environments and suggestive of the native habitat of certain kinds of animal life. Of course, it is more than just copying nature. I am seeking to use the most expressive elements of a given landscape to make compositions which emphasize the intimate relationship between animals and plants. That is, I am trying to show some of the realities of nature by abstracting and accentuating certain aspects, which might be described as the essence of nature rather than the image of nature. The intimate relationship between animal and plant is a constant source of amazement to me, an imperfectly understood mystery. The beaks of hummingbirds for instance, have assumed a form specifically adapted for the extraction of nectar from the flower of a bromeliad or a *Heliconia*. There are also analogies of a pictorial kind: the bracts of some species of *Heliconia* resemble in their shape and color certain characteristics of a parrot or an axe beak. There are countless interrelationships of this sort, which for the serious observer offer unlimited scope for the imagination.

I mentioned earlier that collaboration between specialists is almost a prerequisite for any intelligent interpretation of the natural landscape, in terms of what I might call a constructed landscape. Botanists, ecologists, plant physiologists, zoologists, and so on have collaborated with me and without them I do not believe I could attempt to solve some of the complex problems raised by these large public projects we are presently developing.

I would like to return to a further consideration of the botanical garden. It is firstly a systematic collection, however the plant material is arranged. It also has a didactic or educational function. Research is conducted, studies are made, teaching is undertaken, plants are exchanged, hybrids and special strains are propagated–and the results of these manifold activities have to be communicated to the public. For the present time, the inhabitants of our large cities seem to have a decreasing sensibility about understanding nature, or the complex web of life that nature sustains. Here, for example, is a splendid opportunity to illustrate something of the bewildering variety of nature to emphasize her prolific capacity to adapt and adjust to changing conditions. Here, through comparison and juxtaposition, is the possibility of showing how the variations in a plant are a response to the variations in environment and a poignant expression of the plant's will to survive through adaptation. Thus, amongst the family of Bromeliaceae, by bringing together a *Vriesea* and a *Tillandsia* one is able to observe the curious fact that whereas both plants demand high humidity, the *Vriesea* has fashioned itself so that the water necessary for life is stored within the recesses of the plant in a kind of bowl-shaped container, while the *Tillandsia* obtains its water through the utilization of the water vapor at large in the atmosphere. Or, to take another example, one can study something of the evolution of a plant by observing the many small gradations in different members of a family, say, of *Maranta*–subtle modifications in the form, structure, and color of the leaves.

This process of adaptation, of course, extends beyond the plant and its environment to include all forms of life, the plant and the animal, the animal and its environment, man and nature, man and society. Thus, one becomes able to appreciate that certain manifestations of animal life arise from given environments. In Brazil, for instance, the wolf (*lobo*) with its howl and crooked legs is a natural product of the Cerrado and has assumed this appearance through its search for the fruit of the *Solanum lycocarpum* (known as wolf's fruit)–a splendid example of adaptation to the environment and of the interrelationship of plant and animal life.[3] I should say, in passing, that two-thirds of Brazil is Cerrado, characterized by plants with hairy leaves, which protect not only from the dry heat but also from the blinding light. Brasília is being built in such an environment. To take another example, what uneven intuition guides a certain butterfly to habitually alight on a gray-barked tree from which it is practically indistinguishable? It is verifiable but inexplicable. And what about the many plant associations that are seemingly interdependent, such as the *Mimosa calodendron* which clings to the *Lychnophora* and to the *Anthurium affina?* And what is the explanation for the colossal trunk of the baobab (*Adansonia digitata*) but that it is some adaptation necessary for survival. All of this should remind us that the manifestations of nature are not arbitrary, but the response to given laws which lie outside ourselves and are independent of our wills. And I would like to stress that nature is a symbolic whole,the elements of which are all intimately related–that is, the size of the plant, its form, structure, color, smell, movement, and so on, are not isolated and unrelated phenomena. Within this concept of nature, the plant is no longer a self-contained entity, an object in a collection. It is far more: it is a system endowed with enormous powers of growth and evolution having a *modus vivendi* with the world around it.

Observation of nature is, as I have implied, a tremendous stimulus to the imagination. One finds in nature enlightening analogies–the common spoon resembles the spathe of an Aracea, the fishhook might have evolved from the curved spine of a palm, or perhaps from a *Desmoncus.* Similarly, the very elaborate organization of stresses and forces of the nervous system preexisted in the intricate nerve patterns of the leaves of *Victoria regia.* How strange it is to examine certain primitive art forms only to verify that they are based on the observation of nature! It is almost as if nature had anticipated the thoughts and aspirations of men. It suggests that beauty is not meaningless but fundamentally arises out of a reason for being.

Nature is such an indefatigable teacher! There are lessons to be understood in the distribution of plants and the economy of means and directness with which nature adapts herself to changing conditions. How many times have we noticed on a large surface of green, say, a yellow or red area, and this colored part seemed to satisfy a necessary condition: it was just in the right place; it needed to be there. Nature does not waste time in prevarication, in deciding what to eliminate or what to promote. A plant has a reason for being or it does not survive: the weak and worthless are ruthlessly overcome. Nature places herself above our rather innocent philosophical notions of what is good or what is bad; the laws of nature operate absolutely and inevitably. I must say, on the other hand, that I sometimes tend toward a pantheistic inclination and ask, as do certain Hindu botanists, whether a plant has any feeling, whether it can be exalted, whether it can experience pain, since these all seem to be a part of its life cycle—birth, growth, blooming, fruiting, withering, death. Do not the prolific blossoms on a plant manifest happiness? Sometimes I would like to think so.

I ought to say something about the destruction of nature. In Brazil, we are witnessing a wave of expansion and exploitation which spares little thought for nature. But even though needless destruction is considerable, there is still a vast amount that cannot be destroyed. It seems to me to be almost an obligation of the landscape architect to combat destruction and to preserve certain ill-fated species in danger of extinction, in order that they may survive for the education and enjoyment of future generations.

I have spent a good part of my life enlarging the vocabulary of the landscape architect through the search and introduction of new plants from the hinterland of Brazil. This sort of pioneering effort has demanded some understanding of plant geography, the composition of forest vegetation (from ground covers, undergrowth, and plants of medium height, to tall trees, and epiphytes), some familiarity with natural formations, and a knowledge of the regional distribution of plants. Of course, the biology of the forest is far from being completely understood, and many mysteries remain to challenge and provoke the thoughtful mind. I have learned a good deal about the differentiation of plant communities between different regions.

At São Paulo, I am trying to create ten areas to illustrate the typical ecology of representative regions of Brazil, namely, Amazonas and Pará, south of Bahia, Maranhão and Piauí, the Atlantic coastal mountains behind Rio de Janeiro and São Paulo, Rio Doce, the Campos, the Cerrado, the Caatinga, Paraná, Santa Catarina. The first, Amazonas (the Amazon basin), for example, is a great sea of soft water vegetation. Nature is in a constant state of flux: there are floating islands, chunks of land that break away, and periodic inundations that cover the tops of the tallest trees.

A landscape architect quickly learns that without a knowledge of
the soil, and how it should be treated in light of its excesses or
deficiencies, the construction of a garden may easily result in failure.
He needs to know how various materials may be added to the soil–
sand to give it a looser and more aerated texture, clay to make
it impermeable, peat and humus to enrich, lime to make it more alkaline,
and so on. Nature has her own methods of replenishing soil. In the
forests the falling leaves, the action of roots, the collection of other
loose debris, and the action of the rains all tend toward decomposition
on the forest floor and into a mass of detritus which serves as a layer
of soil completely independent of the underlying geological substrata.

I have mentioned earlier that one may observe in nature the
process of adaptation: plants that are particularly expressive of certain
environments. Another phenomenon is that of succession, the
sequence of plant communities that extend in logical order from the
seashore to the high mountains. There are mangrove swamps,
the Restinga (or shore dunes, a wonderfully interesting habitat which
is fast disappearing in the State of Guanabara), the lagoons and salt
marshes (with their flora of *Bactris setosa* [a spiny palm], samambaia
[common ferns], *Acrostichum aureum* [the golden leather fern],
and the yellow-flowered hibiscus); and then the various forests of the
valleys and foothills, mountain slopes, and mountain tops, exposed
to the hot sun and strong winds, frequently lost in the clouds, and
supporting their own characteristic cloud forest.

I have spoken at some length about the importance of nature, and
an understanding and respect for it. But to avoid misunderstanding,
I want to stress again the distinction I made earlier between the natural
landscape and the constructed landscape, the former created by the
interplay of natural forces and processes (some of which I have touched
upon), the latter the product of the creative and manipulative hand
of man. A balance must be achieved between the two, the one must
complement the other; the garden becomes the transition
between architecture and the greater landscape.

That is why the educational function of a botanical garden
is profoundly important: it illustrates the ways of nature through
comparison and analogy.

1   Frans Post (1612–1680) and Albert
    Eckhout (1610–1665) were Dutch
    painters who traveled to Dutch Brazil
    between 1637 and 1644 to record the
    landscape and people in an expedition
    sponsored by Count Johan Maurits
    van Nassau-Siegen, governor of Dutch
    Brazil. Post's *A Brazilian Landscape,*
    1650, was painted in Haarlem, the
    Netherlands, subsequent to the trip.
    It is now housed in the Metropolitan
    Museum of Art in New York.
2   A German-born naturalist, Georg
    Marcgrave (1610–1644), authored
    Historia Naturalis Brasiliae with Willem
    Piso (1611–1678). They took part
    in the expedition sponsored by van
    Nassau-Siegen.
3   See *Landscapes of Brazil* and
    particularly page 206–8, for more
    on the Cerrado.

The Landscape Architect in the World, Today

Undated English lecture.

Innovation, changes, and new possibilities of expression have led
to a rapid process of urbanization, to a degree never seen before in the
history of mankind. These changes culminate today in a new class of
settlement where the urban complex reaches dimensions which crush
the human and contribute to individualistic isolation. Thus, one
more paradox is established in our contemporary life: millions of people
living one next to the other, without knowing each other or without
any interest, at least, in getting acquainted with their mutual existences;
rather with a feeling that one's enjoyment of the benefits of nature is
limited not by a lack of command of those benefits, but rather by others
who also assert that same right.

These preliminary verifications lead us, planners and organizers
of the natural or urban landscape, to examine the relationship
between our aesthetic experiences and the social and
historical contexts of our time.

The urban organization of cities and of their areas (urbanism-
landscape-architecture), which by their very function act like a
channel or framework for the life of thousands of persons, can no
longer be directed according to procedures or policies which are
not in accordance with the general conditions of modern thinking: the
organization of urban space without considering the modifications
induced in communication, production, and transportation media is
entirely unthinkable.

The revolution in the order of the transformation processes
of matter, which science and technology have engendered, has great
repercussions across centuries.

The revolutionary conditions in communications and transportation
media require vast transformations in the structure of cities and, together
with population growth, they clamor for a renewal in the institutions
which, even in more developed countries, still reflect their rural origin.
The situation appears to be chaos, where urban equipment is not
capable of satisfying the current demand.

The only way to find a solution for the impasse is long and short-
term planning, in order to make it possible, at least, to channel the
potentialities of urban settlements, to better use them for the common
good. This would mean to repeat once more what has been said by

specialists in all fields: to direct the development of settlements without increasing even more their present unbalance. But we don't consider this planning only on literary terms; the many sides of the problem require an integrated cooperation of a large staff of specialists to guide the government's and chiefly the citizens' decisions, either in economic planning or in territorial and urban planning. As for the latter, knowledge of the development history of each settlement is a necessary, important factor *conditio sine qua non* to solve each problem not of the abstract city but of each specific city. The planner will consider each city's history, its joys and sufferings, its tendencies for occupation of the urban soil and its communication media, the places where its inhabitants traditionally gather, its wide-open areas, the green areas which surround the city, and the city's relationship with other cities.

Here, the work of the landscape architect begins. But before we discuss this point, we will talk about some ideas which are necessary to explain our position. Besides the obstacles previously indicated, which require the planner to solve the problem while staying in the background, our work is hindered by a very wrong idea about the functions and field of action of the landscape architect. We wish to point out some fundamental viewpoints: the landscape architect as a creator and organizer of the urban space, who emphasizes the pastoral beauty of the landscape and its components; as a member of the territorial and urban planning staff; and as a scientist guiding his work for the use of regional flora, and contributing efficiently to the maintenance of remaining natural reserves.

In order to make didactic the report on the aspirations and tendencies for landscape architecture within contemporary art and urbanism,[1] we will discuss them separately, so they may be better understood. However, I must make it clear that actually, this relationship is processed simultaneously. When we discuss the specifics of our aesthetic experience, we do not consider it as a separate universe. Art integrates with life; it is a way of thinking and of acting; which generates a specific activity of the spirit and which is closely connected with man's aspirations to express his own view of the world. The experience is based not on an intuitive method, but on a system with a determined, deliberate direction of the proposed artistic problem and of the instruments and techniques adequate for its solution. Thus, we consider art as a power to organize and pre-conceive. It does not merely understand and locate or materialize the general thinking of a community, but rather it creates; not a translation, but an invention; closely tied to human conditions and a necessary and not superfluous activity, even more necessary when we verify that merely mechanical activities have been substituted for machine, in relation to physical effort, or knowledge, or memory, leaving an ever-increasing availability in the life of contemporary man.

Simultaneously with the development of machines, our perceptive power has greatly expanded, making it possible to have a better understanding of the intimate structure of matter, and symbolize it with the microscope; or to explore the cosmos and get better acquainted with it by describing it with the telescope and now with satellites. However, paradoxically, our ability to transmit is limited and much more difficult than it is to explain our position with relation to our art, and talk about it in an adequate manner. The distortions of the language we use force complex and rich content into the narrowness of words, in such a way that every time we wish to give a structural idea of an image, we verify that it is impossible to explain it without using other images, which, however, will not give the exact idea of what we wish to say, making it extremely difficult to communicate the artistic experience. For instance, to name a color, a perfume, a sound, a texture, generally we have only adjectives available, which are parallel images, giving merely close ideas, and this happens only if we think that the content of the parallels we used means the same to our interlocutor as it does to us.

The awareness of this difficulty and of the complex problems of current life present a challenge to our abilities: in order to solve them, and to find a way which may offer possibilities to use the potential that the progress of science and technique offer us for the creativity and functions of today's man, in his task of constructing a better and more peaceful world for everyone.

Man, we may say, has always been gregarious, has always gathered in communities. It is our patient and constant search to create and organize spaces which favor this communion, this desire to understand

and communicate which every man has. The organization of the urban space provides this, because it makes men face each other and the cycle of natural life: birth, the growth of natural plants and animals, their association among themselves and with the mineral formations of the soil, with the various climates, the struggle to adapt themselves to the environment, the blooming and the fall of leaves, the seasons, the changes caused by the sunlight and by rain. We feel this is one of the most urgent tasks of our civilization.

The garden is a link between man and nature, between man and the architecture of open spaces. It is the place where he finds himself, and where he finds respect for the meaning of creation in development. The child learns to behave in front of others and gets acquainted with nature as an aesthetic phenomenon and as a manifestation of life. The youngster finds there the appropriate place for natural expansiveness, and the old man, the place for rest and contemplation. The brutality of the present urban conditions make the garden a compelling necessity, in its most broad significances designed for public and intensive use, when, to the landscaping and plastic aspects of urbanism is integrated the stimulations of being.

The understanding of the existing landscape and the study of the possibilities offered by urbanism are not always considered: the desire to profit and the philosophy of the "minimum necessary" leads to the practice of urbanization formulas, which is to say, of division in lots. The bulldozer levels the land, clearing it all, even any difference in levels which would create an interest and help to render more pleasant the unbearable monotony of the constructions, as for instance when it tears down any existing vegetation which is an obstacle to the linear and unimaginative design made by those responsible for the lotting. After, a few exotic trees are planted and this way they think the problem is solved. The areas between the constructions, so-called gardens, sometimes meet the dimension requirements of the law on green areas, but do not solve the problem as far as the community is concerned.

Le Corbusier, in thinking on this problem, studied the housing units with the purpose of leaving more green space and giving back the soil to the pedestrian.[2] The greens of cities like São Paulo are insignificant, and the same may be said about Rio de Janeiro; in Copacabana, the area with the largest population density in Brazil, the beach relieves the situation of thousands of children and youngsters otherwise squeezed into actual concrete shacks (*favelas*) for their living arrangements.

The problem in North American cities seems to be the same, worsened by the incredible growth of the metropolis, the causes of which we are not going to analyze in this work. We merely verify the phenomenon that the world tends toward a constant increase of demographic indices. We may try to improve the situation by tackling the problem from different angles, always having in view that the city is composed of human groups, of individuals with their anguishes and passions, and that the important thing is to study them in their interrelations to find the equilibrium which will permit them to express themselves as human beings capable of creativity in their pertinent fields.

It is not a static equilibrium, but a search for a dynamic balance, for a harmonious development.

The city is a more or less rigid frame, which makes man resign himself to certain rules with relation to the respect due to others. Rules, which have been made not to include the possibilities of expression of the individual, but to permit an exchange of ideas and to conduct a common work. At the same time, the city—not just the place of work—is the "habitat" of modern man, offering him simultaneously a great variety of choice in his job and in his way of life, together with many difficulties which hamper his creative capacity due to deficient housing facilities, inadequate transportation, noise and sounds which tear him to pieces; not to mention other deeper difficulties in his work relationship, in the opportunities of education, and in the enjoyment of the pleasures the city offers him.

It is also essential for the organizer of urban space to understand social structures and group tendencies; hence the importance of the participation of the sociologist and the economist in the staff for programming and planning, and to construct cities or sections that extend to one another like neighboring units.

We plan for today's man, not for the 21st-century man, but with the necessary flexibility and foresight for areas designed for population growth. However, strict laws should at least impede the proliferation of indiscriminate lots, which require, besides necessary infrastructures, electric and water installations, communications media, etc., also urban supplementations, such as schools, nurseries, libraries, and a plan for green areas adequate to the community. It is not sufficient to plan for appropriate green areas; it is necessary to understand them in relation to the urban landscape and to characterize them by means of a flora peculiar to each region, with ecological and environmental adaptations.

But we have verified that this is not the policy adopted in most cases: the vocabulary used in the garden is monotonous. For instance, in Brazil: it is a country with one of the richest regional floras of the world, with more than 50,000 species, approximately 5,000 trees of great beauty; and in tree planting they use exotic samples, for example almond trees, Australian pines, lignum vitae. Not that we consider these trees ugly, but we only feel that they do not fit in Brazil's landscape. That's why, when we plan a garden in our country, we use the Brazilian flora, adapting it always to the different characteristics of the vegetation, because even among tropical flora there are significant differences depending on the ecological situation. This does not mean that the tropical flora is the only flora which offers us possibilities, due to its richness and exuberance; or that the vibrant colors are its exclusive asset. Nothing is more dazzling than an autumn in the Nordic countries, with its orgy of yellows, oranges, ochres, reds, and browns, setting the landscape afire; or nothing richer in shades than nature in winter: whites, grays, violets, blues, forming a contrast with the dark colors of tree trunks, naked of leaves.

The understanding of the beauty of each region's landscape permits us to give to the garden a valid and peculiar expression: the search for the original in itself does not interest us, and we always try to get rid of prejudice in the evaluation of the vocabulary to be used. But the vocabulary must be thoroughly known, and for this, we have the valuable assistance of a staff of scientists devoted to the study of nature: botanists, ecologists, dendrologists, and others, who help us to correctly express ourselves in the utilization of plants.

It is not necessary for the landscape architect to specialize himself in such fields, first because it is impossible within one lifetime to deeply tackle so many different aspects, unlike the well-known Brazilian botanist Henrique Lahmeyer de Mello Barreto. Also, our worries are already so many that we do not gain much by specializing ourselves in other fields. What interests us is to have an idea of what to ask the specialists, and the manner of using their information. We believe that, in this way, we may improve the existing situation in relation to green urban areas and for the near future, the qualification of professionals who will decisively influence regional and municipal administrations. We feel that the teaching of these fundamental aspects should be emphasized in architecture and urbanism schools, and also in schools which discuss matters relating to botanical and agricultural engineering, in addition to a wide dissemination to the public, to avoid ecological absurdities frequently in evidence.

Although it is necessary, as we mentioned, to qualify the personnel responsible for the preparation, programming, and execution of regional and urban plans, due to the great complexity of the landscape architect's task, we believe that this qualification should be carried out by personnel trained in schools where architecture and urban problems are dealt with, but with emphasis being given specifically to landscape architecture. In brief, we feel it is necessary to increase the study of landscape architecture in appropriate schools established for this purpose. We finish now the presentation of the chief aspects which the landscape architect should discuss in today's world.

1   Originally, "landscaping."
2   Such as Le Corbusier's Unité
    d'habitation in Marseille (1952), a
    "vertical garden city" suspended on
    pilotis above the landscape beneath.

Roberto Burle Marx:
Biographical Notes

1909	Born in São Paulo, August 4
1913	Family moved to Rio de Janeiro
1928–1929	Burle Marx spends eighteen months in Europe
1929	Begins to study painting at the School of Fine Arts in Rio de Janeiro
1932	First garden commission for Schwartz family, Rio de Janeiro
1934–1937	Director of Parks in Recife, Pernambuco
1938	Roof gardens of the Ministry of Education and Health, Rio de Janeiro
1949	Acquired the Sítio at Barra de Guaritiba, south of Rio de Janeiro, and expanded his collection of tropical plants
1954–1964	Flamengo Park, Rio de Janeiro
1955	Founded Burle Marx & Cia. Ltda.
1965	Awarded Fine Arts Medal of the American Institute of Architects
1965, 1988	Ministry for Foreign Affairs, Brasília
1968	Entered partnership with Haruyoshi Ono and José Tabacow
1970	Ministry of Justice, Brasília
1970	Ministry of the Army, Brasília
1970	Copacabana Beachfront, Rio de Janeiro
1979–1992	Fazenda Vargem Grande, Areias, SP
1981	Largo da Carioca, Rio de Janeiro
1982	CESP, Avenida Bela Cintra, São Paulo
1983	Chaim Weizmann Square, Botafogo, Rio de Janeiro
1983	Banca Safra H.Q., Avenida Paulista, São Paulo
1985	Bequeathed the Sítio and collections to the Brazilian nation
1993	Julio de Noronha Square, Leme, Rio de Janeiro
1994	Golden Green, Barra da Tijuca, Rio de Janeiro
1994	Died on June 4 at the Sítio, Barra de Guaratiba, RJ

Gareth Doherty is Associate Professor of Landscape Architecture and Director of the Master in Landscape Architecture Program at the Harvard University Graduate School of Design. He is author of *Paradoxes of Green: Landscapes of a City-State,* published in 2017 by the University of California Press. Previous publications include, *Is Landscape…? Essays on the Identity of Landscape,* edited with Charles Waldheim (Routledge, 2016); and *Ecological Urbanism,* edited with Mohsen Mostafavi (Lars Müller Publishers, 2010, revised in 2016). Doherty is a founding editor of the *New Geographies* journal and editor in chief of *New Geographies 3: Urbanisms of Color.*

Leonardo Finotti is a Brazilian photographer with an international reputation. Whether the results of commissions or his personal initiatives, his photos are published all over the world. His visual research revolves around cities and architecture, with solo and group exhibitions and works shown in important public and private collections. He runs obra comunicação, a collaborative communication office that produces articles, exhibitions, and catalogs. Previous publications include *Futebol* (Lars Müller Publishers, 2014) and *A Collection of Latin American Modern Architecture* (Lars Müller Publishers, 2016).

Acknowledgments

First of all, I have a deep gratitude for Haruyoshi Ono, who graciously welcomed me to Burle Marx & Cia. Ltda. in 1996 and, when I was leaving the studio to return home, presented me with the photocopies of lectures from which this collection originated. Many years later, Haruyoshi entrusted me with the formidable responsibility of editing Roberto's voice in the publication of these lectures. I also draw from several interviews with Haruyoshi in the introduction. Without Haruyoshi's genorosity, kindness, and confidence in me this volume would never have happened. This book is dedicated to Haru.

Dating from my initial trip to Brazil in 1996, there are many people to thank, including my friends Isabela Ono, Júlio Ono, Gustavo Leivas, and Duarte Vaz, with whom I remain in contact to this day. This book was completed with their support and with the help of Gisela Nina of the studio, as well as Claudia Maria Pinheiro Storino, of IPHAN and Sítio Roberto Burle Marx.

I first traveled to Brazil and Venezuela in 1996 on a travel scholarship from the Royal Horticultural Society in London. My intention was to compare the work of Roberto Burle Marx with the work of Sir Geoffrey Jellicoe. In the introduction, I draw from a series of interviews I had with Jellicoe. Jellicoe encouraged me to study Burle Marx based not just on my academic interests, but on the nature of the curves he created in his work. Hans Broos, Riberio Dias, Maru Gomes, Regina Lemgruber Julianele, Oswaldo de Nehry, Jorge Sakai, and John G. Stoddart were all very generous with their time during that initial trip to South America.

Eighteen years later, another grant, from the Graham Foundation for Advanced Studies in the Fine Arts, was to allow work on this edited volume to begin. I thank Sarah Herda, James Pike and Stephanie Whitlock, who were incredibly helpful and supportive along the way. Without this grant, and the support of the Graham Foundation, these lectures probably never would have been published.

Support for editing the lectures was provided by the John D. Scruggs Traveling Fellowship and Research Fund in Landscape Architecture at the Harvard University Graduate School of Design (GSD). I acknowledge the kind support of my department chair, Anita Berrizbeitia, professor of landscape architecture at the GSD, herself a scholar of Burle Marx. Other colleagues who helped in so many ways include Francesca Benedetto, Silvia Benedito, Danielle Choi, Sonja Dümpelmann, Steven Handel, Gary Hilderbrand, Mohsen Mostafavi, Paul Nakazawa, Pat Roberts, Susan Nigra Snyder, George E. Thomas, and Melissa Vaughn, now of MIT, who advised on the initial stages of the project. Archival research was generously facilitated by Ines Zalduendo, Special Collections Archivist and Reference Librarian, and Sarah Willoughby Dickinson, Research Support Services Librarian, Frances Loeb Library, Harvard Graduate School of Design; Myles Crowley, Reference Associate, MIT Institute Archives and Special Collections was very helpful too.

I thank John Beardsley and Kathryn Moore for their friendship and for their advice at various stages of this publication process. Several colleagues discussed sometimes tiny but significant details and helped with finding images or in reading drafts of the manuscript. They include Caroline Constant, Marina Correia, Fábio Duarte, Mariano Gomez Luque, Miguel Lopez Melendez, Stephen J. Ramos, and Catherine Seavitt Nordenson.

Various research assistants helped along the way, most of all William Baumgardner, who has the capacity for finding needles in haystacks in record time. Abner Luis Calixter, Rajji Sanjay Desai, Mariana Pereira Guimarães, Jian He, A. J. Sus, and Felipe Vera all helped at various points of the research and editing.

Jason Dyett and Manoel Pereira Neto, both formerly of the David Rockefeller Center for Latin American Studies' Harvard Brazil Office in São Paulo welcomed me on my research trips.

The copy editing of these lectures was carefully and cheerfully undertaken by Jane Acheson, to whom I remain indebted for her patience and good company and for another completed project. Joana Canedo compared the English translations with the original Portuguese. Melissa Harkin provided translations from Portuguese. I thank Carolyn Wheeler and Keonaona Peterson for their precise proofreading, and Tobiah Waldron for completing the index.

Thanks to Leonardo Finotti for the remarkable photographic essay on Roberto Burle Marx and for shooting new photographs especially for this book. Alex Souza assisted Leonardo in this process. I especially enjoyed our site visits together.

My cousin, Margaret O'Doherty, first introduced me to the work of Roberto Burle Marx. Cathal Doherty SJ accompanied me on my first trip to Brazil. Moisés Lino e Silva accompanied me on my subsequent trips to Brazil.

I thank Lars Müller Publishers, and especially Lars Müller, Martina Mullis, Alice Poma, and Maya Rüegg, for their creativity and professionalism. Lars Müller believed in this project from moment I first mentioned it, and agreed to publish this volume even when it was still a collection of photocopies stored in a file in Ireland. Together we visited several of Burle Marx's landscapes in Brazil and met with Haruyoshi and Isabela Ono in Rio de Janeiro. Lars's craft and attention to the detail of building books is reflected in the attitude of his team in Zurich. It has been an honor to collaborate with such a talented team dedicated to the design and publishing of beautiful books.

And I thank Günther Vogt for his quiet and determined generosity and unwavering encouragement for this project. Günther has that all-too-rare combination of art and botanical knowledge, akin to Burle Marx's, which creates a powerful landscape architecture as a complement to cities and society. Günther's support made this book a physical reality.

GD

Photographs by Leonardo Finotti

32
Banco Safra, roof garden
São Paulo, 1983

33
FIESP, wall relief
São Paulo, 1979

34
Praça Rodrigues de Abreu
São Paulo, 1990

35
Parque Cultural Paulista
São Paulo, 1986

36
Centro de Processamento
de Dados do Banco do Brasil
São Paulo, 1970

37–38
Parque Burle Marx
(formerly Pignatari residence)
São Paulo, 1956

39
Fazenda Vargem Grande
Areias, SP, 1979–1991

40
Parque das Mangabeiras
Belo Horizonte, 1980

41
Faculdade de Arquitetura
e Urbanismo (UFRJ)
Rio de Janeiro, 1961

42–43
Praça Chaim Weismann
Rio de Janeiro, 1983

44
Sheraton Hotel, roof garden
Rio de Janeiro, 1968

45–46
BNDES
Rio de Janeiro, 1974

47
Petrobras
Rio de Janeiro, 1969

48–49
Largo da Carioca
Rio de Janeiro, 1981

50
Museu de Arte Moderna (MAM)
Rio de Janeiro, 1954

51–53
Flamengo Park
Rio de Janeiro, 1954–1964

54–56
Parque del Este
Caracas, 1956–1961

57–58
Sítio Santo Antônio da Bica
Barra de Guaratiba, RJ, 1949–1994

ESPAÇO FRANCISCANO · FRANCISCAN SP

Roberto Burle Marx Lectures
Landscape as Art and Urbanism

Editor: Gareth Doherty
Photography: Leonardo Finotti
Copyediting: Jane Acheson (engl.),
Joana Cranedo (port.)
Proofreading: Keonaona Peterson, Carolyn Wheeler
Translations: Melissa Harkin, Moisés Lino e Silva
Coordination: Maya Rüegg
Design: Integral Lars Müller/Lars Müller and
Alice Poma
Production: Esther Butterworth
Lithography: prints professional, Berlin, Germany
Printing and binding: Graspo, Zlín, Czech Republic
Paper: Qutro Silk, 135 gsm and
Munken Print White 15, 115 gsm

Lars Müller Publishers
Pfingstweidstrasse 6
8005 Zurich, Switzerland
+41 44 274 37 40
info@lars-mueller-publishers.com
www.lars-mueller-publishers.com

Product safety
Producer: Lars Müller Publishers GmbH
Responsible person in accordance with EU
Regulation 2023/988 (GPSR): Michael Klein,
sales representative, Hub 1, DE-84149 Velden
+49 8742 964 552 2
gpsr@lars-mueller-publishers.com

ISBN 978-3-03778-625-3

Distributed in North America, Latin America
and the Caribbean by ARTBOOK | D.A.P.
www.artbook.com

Printed in the Czech Republic

Image Credits

Photos 1–58: © Leonardo Finotti
Figs. a–g: © Burle Marx & Cia. Ltda.,
Rio de Janeiro

Inside front cover: Roberto Burle Marx during
his lunchtime address to the annual meeting
of the American Association of Landscape
Architects (ASLA), 1985
© Burle Marx & Cia. Ltda., Rio de Janeiro

Inside back cover: *Heliconia burle-marxii*,
illustration by Margaret Mee, 1970
Watercolor on Fabriano paper, 26 × 19 in
(66 × 48 cm)
© Sítio Roberto Burle Marx, IPHAN/MinC

A grant from the Graham Foundation for
Advanced Studies in the Fine Arts facilitated
the photographic essays by Leonardo Finotti,
image reproduction rights, archival research,
and editing. The book's first printing and
publication was generously supported by
VOGT Landscape